Advance Praise for
Imperfect Harmony

"This book is a great contribution to the literature. It will significantly help people think carefully and thoughtfully about their marriages. In addition, it is the first book to provide clinicians with tools to help their patients sort through the complex choices facing many individuals and couples: How and when do you stay in a marriage because of the children? What can you do to maximize your happiness and the happiness of children under these circumstances? How much of your own psychology is contributing to the difficulties in your marriage and your dissatisfaction with life? Under what circumstances does it make sense to leave? This book offers clear and concrete help navigating these challenging and important questions that plague so many couples and individuals."

> —*Jessica Broitman, Ph.D., Faculty, San Francisco Psychoanalytic Institute, Wright Institute, Executive Director, San Francisco Psychotherapy Training Center, and Vice President, San Francisco Psychotherapy Research Group*

"Dr. Coleman has successfully managed to bring the reader beyond the black-and-white debate of marriage versus divorce into the rich grays of relationship and parenting. Drawing from years of clinical practice and an impressive literature review from the fields of psychology, biology, and anthropology, he has brought us a text that will appeal to a public desperate for new ideas about how to stay married with children. His book will also be invaluable to health-care professionals eager to deepen their understanding of this complex topic."

> —*Dale C. Dallas, M.D., Chief of Physician Wellness, Associate Chief, Mental Health and Chemical Dependency Services, Kaiser Permanente Medical Center*

"This is a profound book about reality in life and marriage. Writing in beautiful prose and using wonderful examples, Dr. Coleman helps the reader understand the subtleties of marital conflict and their effect on children. While it is written for men and women, it is rare to see a man writing with such sensitivity and compassion about the way women think and feel. I also love this book because it presents a sophisticated way to understand the workings of the self that is practical and intuitive. In that sense, it is an even larger and more important book than the title promises and provides valuable reading for anyone."

—*Heather Folsom, M.D., psychiatrist and author*

"An original and provocative approach to the universal dilemma of what to do about the well-being of children in a less-than-wonderful marriage. This book can be of great help to couples who are struggling with these issues."

—*Susan Forward, Ph.D., author of* Emotional Blackmail *and* Toxic In-Laws

"This book is a first, a first to help parents understand that divorce is not the only solution for the problems facing those married with children. The arrival of children is always a monumental relationship challenge, but Dr. Coleman humorously and with detailed anecdotes helps those parents ride the wave of discontent and arrive at the ultimate truth: the grass is not always greener on the other side. The journey leads the reader to understand that the pursuit of happiness at any time and with any relationship is inextricably linked to self-reflection. I loved this book."

—*Rolleen Kent McIlwrath, Judge of the Superior Court, County of San Joaquin, California*

"This is a much-needed book about one of the most important issues of our time. Combining the findings of social research with the wisdom of a professional marriage counselor, Joshua Coleman tells what to do when your marriage is not working out but you realize that staying together for the children is one of the best things you can do for them."

—*David Popenoe, Ph.D., Professor of Sociology and Co-Director, National Marriage Project, Rutgers University*

Imperfect
Harmony

Imperfect Harmony

How to Stay Married
for the Sake of Your Children
and Still Be Happy

JOSHUA COLEMAN, Ph.D.

ST. MARTIN'S PRESS
New York

www.stmartins.com

ISBN 0-312-28974-X

First Edition: July 2003

1 3 5 7 9 10 8 6 4 2

To the Reader

Contents

Foreword

THIS IS A radical book. It challenges some of the most dearly held American beliefs about marriage and long-term relationships. It challenges adults to examine themselves and their marriages for ways to change in order to remain good parents and viable family units for their children. It assumes, in a matter-of-fact, professional, and upbeat manner, that it's desirable and possible to overcome or learn to live with serious relational problems that most in our modern culture would consider grounds for separation and divorce. And it offers the astounding idea that having a marriage characterized by such "imperfect harmony" can be part of a satisfying, happy life.

Dr. Coleman gets right to the heart of the matter in the first chapter, with the statement "Expecting to find happiness in marriage is a bad idea." While marriage has the potential to contribute to one's happiness, he points out the fallacy of expecting a modern marriage with children in a hectic, stressful world to be the wellspring and main source of life's happiness. Carefully exploding the American myth of marriage as "a one-stop shopping center for all your needs," he separates the early stages of infatuation and sexual excitement from mature love, for which he feels most people have little preparation, and of which they have unrealistic expectations.

Useful for both laypeople and professionals, this is a book that helps adults balance their desire to remain a central, full-time parent to their children, and their need for a satisfactory, fulfilling life. From his perspective as a divorced and remarried father, and as a professional in the field, Dr. Coleman points out that many who left marriages in hopes that greater happiness could be found in yet another relationship spend years regretting their actions. One of the hugest regrets is the loss of full-time involvement with children. The comforting homily children are offered when parents separate—adults divorce each other, but parents can never divorce their kids—doesn't hold in real postdivorce life, where parent-child relationships are profoundly altered. It's not just for the sake of the children, but also for their own feelings of fulfillment in remaining central, connected, and fully committed to their children's lives, that parents decide to remain married.

The practical value of the book is in its balance between urging people to work on themselves and their relationship and in helping to develop a new and more realistic perspective on what cannot be changed. Various types of serious relational issues are presented through case examples and through relevant research. These range from the well known (extramarital affairs, high conflict and abuse, sexual incompatibility) to more subtle problems (depression, outgrowing your partner, and how one's past can interfere). Strategies and exercises are offered together with clinical examples to illustrate how these issues can be addressed or how one's perspective can be altered so that the problem seems less painful and more manageable. There are numerous examples and suggestions for how to come to terms with what you have, and learn to accrue satisfaction from multiple sources.

There's little debate that children are better off when their parents stay together, except when marital problems overcome the parents' ability to protect their children. The ongoing high divorce rate is producing generations of young people who have wistful fantasies of being in long-term marriages and giving their children what they never had but who have no workable, realistic models for what it takes to make marriage and parenting work. This situation presents parents in less than ideal marriages with a painful dilemma: remaining married for the sake of the children versus their adult wish to pursue personal happiness. This book offers a radically different approach in that it assumes a perfect or even a great marriage is not essential to either the child's or the adult's well-being. Working to stay together to honor marital and parental commitment and learning to achieve happiness and satisfaction from within and outside the marriage benefits you and shows your kids how to do it.

—JULIA M. LEWIS, PH.D.
Professor of Psychology, San Francisco State University
Coauthor, with Judith Wallerstein, Ph.D.,
and Sandra Blakesle, *The Unexpected Legacy of Divorce:
A Twenty-five-Year Landmark Study*

Introduction

THERE ARE A lot of books on how to have a great marriage. This isn't one of them. This book is about how to live a happy life, regardless of the state of your marriage. Despite the promises of therapists, clergy, and self-help authors, not every relationship can be made better. Some couples are too mismatched by need or temperament to have the kind of intimacy that a good marriage can provide. On the other hand, almost everyone considers the idea of divorce at some point in the relationship; feeling hopeless and discouraged isn't proof that your marriage is flawed or your happiness is doomed.

If there weren't kids, divorce might be a more reasonable option. You could say, "Thanks for the memories" (or the headaches), walk away, and never see him or her again; file lessons learned under "What Was I Thinking?" circa 1993–2003. But, since you're reading this book, you probably have kids and have decided that that option is something you'd rather not choose. You know you can divorce if you have to, but you also know that could damage or destroy what you hold the most dear, your life with them.

Contrary to the wisdom of pop psychology, it is not essential to your or your children's well-being for you to have a great marriage.[1]

Many well-adjusted children have come from homes where the parents were not in love or where the parents weren't well matched. In addition, most children would prefer that their parents stay together even if the parents don't feel fulfilled, as long as there isn't regular, intense fighting in the home. And often, even then.

On the other hand, it isn't enough to stay together just for their sake. You have to stay married in a way that protects them from out-of-control conflicts and arguments. Staying together for your children means showing them how to achieve happiness and satisfaction in life, even when you're not feeling fulfilled by your partner; it means staying together and being a good friend to your children despite the conflict that's occurring between you and your spouse. This book will show you the strategies to achieve this.

While this is a book about staying together, it's not a book against divorce. Sometimes people feel so suffocated, trapped, or harmed by their marriages that divorce is the best option, even if the kids would be better off with the parents together. Some feel it was worth it to achieve a more successful marriage, or to escape from a difficult partner (see Ahrons 1994; Hetherington 2002). In some cases, where the conflict is frequent and harmful to the children, both parents *and* children may be better off if the parents split up.[2]

On the other hand, some people break up and spend the rest of their lives thinking it was the stupidest thing they ever did. They weren't able to fully appreciate what they had until it was gone. And they can't get it back again. Ever. Among other things, this book will give you the tools to see where you are on this continuum and how best to proceed.

My interest in this topic stems from my own experience, both personally and professionally. I was married and divorced in my twenties and now have a twenty-two-year-old daughter from that marriage. I became remarried fourteen years ago and have twin ten-year-old boys. I have been able to give my sons the precious resource of what I could never give my first child: day-to-day, minute-to-minute parenting.

Divorce creates all kinds of cracks in a parent's and child's life that have to be constantly tended and mended. You can miss a lot in a day. Being a part-time parent bears little resemblance to a full-time family. I'm grateful that my daughter and I are close, but nothing can replace the days that I lost with her by being a part-time father. I wish I could tell you that I no longer have any sadness about it, but I can't. I would rather you take what I say as testimony from the other side and use it to appreciate the strength and treasure of raising your children full-time. A life with children may not seem like the center of your universe when you're in the midst of being in a difficult marriage, but it can feel like everything when it's gone (Coleman 2002b).

Besides, the decision to stay married for the sake of your children isn't just for your children. It's also something you do for yourself.[3] You stay together because you know that nothing can replace the experience of waking up to them, watching their daily struggles and victories, helping them navigate the playground politics when they're younger, and keeping them on the right path when they enter the teenage world of alcohol, drugs, and sex. You get to tuck them into bed every night, not just the nights when it's your turn because the other parent just had them for the past few days or weeks or months. Also, you don't have the guilt of wondering how the divorce is affecting them and whether they'll be harmed in the ways you've been reading so much about.

While nothing prepares us for what marriage is going to be like, the same can be said of divorce with children. People often tell their kids, "Daddy and Mommy are getting divorced, but parents don't get a divorce from their children." When you get divorced and your child comes back and forth, in and out of your life, you discover that's not entirely true.

I have written this book with three aims:

1. *to give you the tools to determine whether your marriage can be bettered;*

xvii

2. *to give you the tools to enjoy your life if your marriage can't be bettered;*

3. *to help you protect your children from whatever is unsatisfying or difficult in your life or marriage.*

Most individuals and couples come to therapy in some state of hopelessness, much as I imagine you're in right now. It is not at all unusual for someone to enter therapy on the verge of divorce and discover a renewed sense of joy and interest in the marriage several weeks or months later; *sometimes* things can seem hopeless in a marriage when there's still lots that can be done to fix it. My job is to help you determine whether you feel hopeless because you're in a state of normal gridlock or because there really isn't much that can be done about your differences for now, or maybe forever more. If the latter is the case, my job is to help you begin to make peace with that or start considering other options. Understanding the possibilities and limitations of your marriage is critical to your well-being and the well-being of those around you because it influences your decisions, your mood, and your behavior. Knowing where you stand will help you decide how you want to structure your life and marriage going forward.

The ability to stay married for the sake of your children requires a different strategy and outlook than what is normally prescribed in the marital self-help literature. This book is written to provide you with new ways to think and feel about yourself and your marriage, and to galvanize you into action. It is written for anyone who is looking for guidance on how to remain married during those times when everything seems to be going out, and nothing is coming back. It's written for those who are ready to call it quits but know that others are counting on them to keep it going. It is written for those who are weighted down with loneliness and envy of all of the seemingly happy couples who don't have to struggle so much to make things work. And whether for the long term or the short term, it is written to help you discover how to stay married for the sake of your children and still be happy.

Imperfect
Harmony

1

Marriage Under Pressure

Isn't my marriage supposed to make me happy?

"My husband and I barely see each other. By the time the kids are in bed we both collapse in a heap and go to sleep. When we do see each other we usually get into an argument about money, or housework, or the kids. I just don't know what I'm getting out of all of this."
—ADRIENNE, AGE THIRTY

MARYANN* WAS A TALL, attractive woman who worked as an office manager for a San Francisco accounting firm. On the phone, she said she wanted to get into therapy to get control of her anxiety. In our first session, Maryann observed that most of her anxiety appeared to be centered around her marriage. She jokingly observed that the only time she didn't seem to be depressed or anxious was when her husband was out of town. "You'd love him if you met him," she said about her husband, Jeff, a local university professor. "He's the most charming, funny person you'd ever want to meet. He knows everything about everything." Her tone revealed a hint of irritation.

"As in know-it-all everything?" I asked, following the irritation.

She laughed. "Definitely as in know-it-all. But also, he really does know a lot. The other night we were out to dinner with friends and somehow we ended up talking about gravity, of all things, and he starts telling the formula for how fast things fall to earth. And that's not even what he teaches."

---

*All of the cases discussed in this book have been carefully disguised to protect patient confidentiality.

"Sounds pretty smart," I said. "What's he like when he's home and not out with friends?" I asked.

"A tyrant!" she said forcefully, as if relieved to finally say it out loud. "That's what's so confusing. Everybody thinks he's Mr. Wonderful because in public he's so charming, but at home, he's impossible. I can't *stand* him." She quickly looked up as if this would offend me. I nodded as if to say that this was not something I was unaccustomed to hearing, since it's not something I'm unaccustomed to hearing.

Her eyes became teary. "The other night, I cut my hand making him dinner and I cried out, it hurt so badly. I'm standing there bleeding with my hand in the sink and he starts telling me to be quiet because I'm distracting him while he's writing out some acceptance speech. I said 'Jeff, I just cut my hand and I'm bleeding in the sink.' He said, 'So just run some water over it and stop bitching about it. You're not a three-year-old, figure it out.' It's like, if it doesn't have to do with him or his career, he's not interested." She went on to describe him as equally uninvolved with the children.

I asked if they had considered couple's therapy and she said that he refused because he didn't think there was anything wrong with him. "He just says that he knows more than any therapist so why should I waste his money? And of course, it's always *his* money even though I work full-time and have full-time responsibility for the house and kids."

Whether or not marriage is the central complaint, I strive to have a good understanding of what my individual clients' marriages are like, who their spouses are, and why they are married to them. I wondered about Jeff as Maryann spoke. On the face of her description, he sounded pretty self-centered and difficult; I could see why she was having problems with him. On the other hand, I wondered if Maryann contributed to his attitude with her own communication or behavior. In that scenario, Jeff's self-centeredness could be an angry expression of feeling neglected and devalued by her, or it could be some other indirect complaint. A destructive style of communication often develops in marriages where couples haven't found a productive way to manage their hurts and differences; because they're not direct with their complaints, a slow and steady pattern of stonewalling and sniping evolves. Before long, both are living behind an electrified fence of resentment and contempt.

Over the next few sessions, I asked Maryann about Jeff's childhood so that I could better help her understand his psychology, and to refine my assessment of their marriage. I learned that he had grown up in a home where he was constantly coddled. He was the only child of parents who had struggled for years with infertility. When they finally had Jeff, they were so happy to have a child that they gave him whatever he demanded. His father, also a professor, idealized him but treated his mother with derision. Jeff's childhood left him feeling entitled to be given to in relationships without making an effort at reciprocating.

Jeff was fifty and Maryann was forty. Their marriage had in many ways been less troubled when their children were small, as Maryann had been a stay-at-home mom and the division of labor and responsibilities had seemed clearer to both of them. In addition, this arrangement had closely mirrored what they both had seen growing up, so neither thought to question it.[1] Problems often surface, however, when there is a change in one of the partners and a change in roles. When the kids entered junior high, Maryann decided to go back to work and felt an increase in independence and self-esteem from doing so. However, she continued to do the same amount of housework and child care without Jeff's involvement. Their marriage began to experience conflict as Maryann sought more help and participation from Jeff.

I saw in Jeff a phenomenon that I often see in my practice: men raised in traditional families have a harder time making the transition to a more egalitarian household when their wives go back to work, or when their wives insist on more equality in the marriage. Because these husbands grew up with a *Father Knows Best* sensibility, they have little personal experience of sharing power and decision making in a family. They are often bewildered by their wife's desire for increased intimacy and power sharing, and often respond with withdrawal, contempt, or hostility.

In addition, men's socialization to be more remote with their emotions makes many of them unable or unwilling to do the kind of self-reflection and disclosure that would make their wives feel cherished and understood (see Real 2002). While I strongly believe that men are as capable of intimacy as women, many need help in learning how to be decent husbands and, sometimes, fathers. Jeff is a more extreme example of this phenomenon, but he's not a rarity. Men like Jeff are not unusual, because our society prizes entitlement and self-involvement in its men. Men who don't "perform" are more likely to find themselves off the fast track of promotions, career advancement, and desirable romantic partners.

This isn't to say that the marital stresses and trade-offs for the genders are equal. Marriage in America is harder for most women with children than it is for men. As author Ann Crittenden writes in *The Price of Motherhood,* men still control the purse strings in the majority of households, and wives typically have much more to lose financially from a divorce than the average husband. This means that women who are in difficult marriages and want to demand more from their husbands often have less with which to negotiate.[2] In addition, women still do the vast majority of child care and housework, even when they work outside the home (Hochschild 1997) and even when their husbands identify their marriages as egalitarian (Gottman 1994).

Women are more likely to be affected by stresses in the family and to respond to those stresses with depression or physical illnesses (Kiecolt-Glaser and Newton 2001). One researcher found that among men and women employed outside the home, contributing more than 46 percent of the total domestic labor in the household greatly increased the symptoms of depression. Thus, one of the reasons that women have twice the incidence of depression as men may be that wives contribute up to 53 percent or more to the domestic chores, whereas husbands' contributions fall well below that (Bird 1999).

Time-use surveys show that as women enter the workplace they take on the equivalent of two full-time jobs. This estimated eighty hour workweek typically forces them to cut back on everything in their lives except paid work and caring for their children (Crittenden 2001). In *The Time Bind: When Work Becomes Home and Home Becomes Work,* sociologist Arlie Hochschild observes that half of all mothers are now working full-time and 55 percent earn half or *more* of the family income. Women are now as likely as men to be part of the 8 percent of workers who hold down two jobs.[3]

It's hard, however, for *anyone* to stay married these days. Couples are constantly being pumped up with billboard-sized expectations of what marriage should be like, while social and economic changes make them less likely than ever to fulfill those expectations. Most of the individuals and couples I see in my practice these days are exhausted. Americans are putting in longer work hours than workers of any other industrialized nation (Hochschild 1997). Between 1960 and 1986 the amount of time that parents had available for their children fell ten hours per week in white households and twelve hours per week in black households, and it continues falling (Fuchs 1988, in Hochschild 1997).

While there has been a shrinking of time, there has been an increased awareness of what constitutes good parenting. Thus, many conscientious parents are devoting much more quality time, if not quantity time, to their children than prior generations (Crittenden 2001). However, this is often at the expense of their own care (Ehrensaft 1997) and the care of their marriages. While the culture appears to have shifted from a parent-centered house to a child-centered house, one of the costs may be a decrease in prioritizing the needs of the couple.

Despite Americans' working harder than ever, fewer and fewer feel economically secure. We have fewer vacation days than in 1970 and increasingly fewer health benefits (Coontz 1997). The stock market is the lowest it has been in three decades, and many large corporations are going belly-up or are under criminal investigation. These economic anxieties directly translate into the marital realm.

In this new world, parents have less time to relax with their children, and couples have less time to focus on their marriages. This tremendous pressure compromises our capacity to be intimate or sensitive to each other's needs. It leaves individuals feeling needy and unfulfilled and vulnerable to fantasies of a more perfect partner who would be sensitive to how much we're doing and how little we're getting back. It makes the challenge of being married, in some ways, more challenging than at any other period of history.

Marriages are also being affected by the outdated memories of our parents' examples as husbands and wives, mothers and fathers. These stressors directly contributed to the problems in Maryann and Jeff's marriage. Despite working a full-time job, Jeff did little to help her organize the household, get the kids fed, help them with their homework, or get them to bed.[4] As she once said to me, "By the end of the weekend, my attitude is Thank God it's Monday."

Many of the husbands I work with have to be taught to become more empathetic toward and involved in the lives of their wives. I certainly did. When my twins were born, my wife and I agreed that I would increase my practice and take on more of the financial responsibilities so that she could be home with the children more. While having twins and a daughter was enough of a stress, we also struggled with the division of labor when both of us were home. Ellie wanted me to pitch in equally with parenting and housework, and my tender attitude was, "Hey, I put in a hard day at the office, you don't have to work full-time, why should I have to go to work and then work as hard when I get home?" I had the memory of my father with his feet propped up and a newspaper on his lap asking my mother when dinner was going to be ready.

Neither my wife nor I knew what was fair to ask or refuse in a situation where she worked part-time and had primary responsibility for the house and children. Despite the fact that she was also a psychologist, she felt uncomfortable insisting on more help from me, having been raised in a home where her mother ran the house and took care of her and her two siblings. Even though our marriage wasn't traditional before our twins, in the sense that we both worked and made decisions equally, having children turned all of that on its head. In other words, we fell into the trap that I see so many couples falling into, where I was acting out of the same sense of entitlement as my male forebears, and she with the lack of entitlement of her female role models.

As a columnist for *TWINS* magazine and a contributor to the *San Francisco Chronicle,* I get frantic letters every week from mothers wanting to know how to get their partners to be more involved as husbands and fathers. I occasionally get letters from fathers wanting to know how to get their wives less focused on the kids and more focused on the marriage again. Both genders want to know if they should leave their marriages, accept this newer and less satisfying arrangement, or force their spouses into therapy.

IMPERFECT HARMONY

MY CREDO AS a psychologist is that no one is hopeless. However, from your perspective as a spouse, your partner might be. Some personality types, like Jeff's let in a lot less light than do others. Sometimes the difference between a satisfying marriage and a marriage for the sake of the children hinges on whether the individuals involved are willing to work on themselves.

Husbands like Jeff are more difficult because they often refuse individual or couple treatment. Or they finally agree to therapy as their wives are serving them with divorce papers, since three out of four times it's the wife who initiates a divorce (Ahrons 1994; Hetherington 2001; Amato and Booth 1997). Or even if they stay, so much foul water may have passed under the bridge that their wives have long ago written them off as a lost cause. If Maryann could get Jeff into couple treatment, I'd work to help him understand the impact of his behavior on his marriage. I'd want him to see that he was unconsciously identified with a narcissistic father. I'd help him understand that his parents were unable to model how much reciprocity the average modern marriage requires. I'd show him how to empathize with Maryann and discover that there are rewards to an intimate level of connection and an equal sharing of child care and housework that are well worth the increase in vulnerability and the decrease in power, as he knew it. *If* I could get him into therapy and *if* he wouldn't quit.

If I worked with them in couple's therapy, I'd help Maryann to see how she colludes in their dynamic by overfunctioning in their home life by taking care of everyone in the family and not insisting on more help and respect from her husband or children. I'd help her to feel less afraid to tell Jeff directly what she wants or doesn't want. I would encourage her to begin refusing to do more for him than is fair for her to do. I would help her to appreciate what is valuable in Jeff and his contributions to the family. I would want both members of the couple to see how they keep the negative fires burning through the use of shame, withdrawal, and resentment.

Unfortunately, Jeff refused to get into individual or marital therapy, and this left Maryann with fewer choices (I'll discuss when and how to use ultimatums in chapter 8). For the most part, he remained self-centered in his stance with her over the course of the two years that I worked with her. However, Maryann became increasingly successful at maintaining her mood, self-esteem, and sense of control over her life and her parenting. While her marriage remained far from ideal, she found a way to maintain happiness and raise her kids in an intact family by using the following strategies. She:

1. *Accepted that Jeff probably would not change.* This means she had to learn to empathize with who he is, grieve for what she wouldn't have in her marriage with him, and eliminate behaviors designed to make him change such as pleading, placating, being overly responsible for his care, and communicating in a passive-aggressive fashion.

2. *Learned to reinterpret his bullying as fragility and self-centeredness*

rather than as a reasonable way for him to behave with her. This step was very confusing to Maryann because Jeff's behavior so closely mirrored her father's treatment of her and her mother.

3. *Developed her own authority in the household so that she wasn't constantly deferring to his demands and entitlement.* This involved becoming more assertive and becoming more conscious of her belief system, which served to shame and scare her out of appropriately self-interested behavior.

4. *Learned to intervene more when Jeff was being critical or hurtful to the children.* This required talking more with Jeff before and after incidents with the children and interrupting him if he was being overly critical.

5. *Developed a plan to increase her involvement in pleasurable activities outside of the home.* This meant increasing her time with her friends and family and developing more hobbies. She also had to work on her guilt about appropriately prioritizing her needs over those of her family's.

6. *Worked on the beliefs that made her vulnerable to guilt, anxiety, and depression.* This meant becoming more conscious of her dysfunctional beliefs and developing positive counter-statements to such beliefs as:

- I don't deserve to be treated well.
- Jeff's happiness is more important than mine.
- It will be terrible if I disappoint him.
- It's my fault if he's unhappy.
- It's better to keep the peace than to push for my own needs.
- It's a woman's responsibility to care for the kids and home (even if she's also working outside the home).

The goals that I developed to help Maryann would be useful for you if your partner has these traits. I will go into *much* more detail about how to achieve these goals in the upcoming chapters, as well as describe other strategies for staying married for the sake of your children in a variety of marriages. Each problem requires a unique plan based on your situation, your personality, and the personality of your partner.

However, one of the first things to understand is the role that expectations play in marriage. It's crucial to understand your expectations of marriage because they may be generating irrational feelings of entitlement to demand the unreasonable and to feel disappointed in the expectable. Irrational expectations may not, on the surface, feel as if they're influencing your beliefs and emotions; however, they may well underlie some of the discontent you feel about your marriage.

IRRATIONAL EXPECTATIONS

ANDY WARHOL SAID that everybody gets fifteen minutes of fame (Warhol 1988). The marital version is that we get three to six months of unconditional love before our relationship starts to falter. The first blush of romance, if we are lucky enough to have one, is driven by a combination of good behavior and biology. On the behavioral side, our desire to make a good impression causes us to roll out our fashionable fall line of strengths, casually displaying an ability to be sensitive, interested, a good provider, a good lover, a good listener, a great friend. On the other hand, we hide from ourselves and our partners that we also have a large, rumpled clothing bag filled with conflicts around intimacy, boundaries, vulnerability to anxiety or depression, issues around money, substances, or body image, problems accessing or controlling emotions—the list continues.

It's probably easiest to hide our flaws and ignore the other's in the beginning because nature is so excited to get us together. At the prospect of having two more subjects to perpetuate one of her species, she provides an intoxicating neuronal elixir of phenylethylamine, norepinephrine, and dopamine (Walsh 1991). These agents provide a biological sales pitch of perfect fulfillment that would shame the most conniving car salesman. Phenylethylamine (PEA) is a naturally occurring amphetamine that, among other things, may account for some of the antidepressant and energizing qualities of exercise (Szabo, Billet, and Turner 2001). It appears to have a powerful effect on nonhumans, too. Mice behave in an exhilarated way when injected with PEA, and rhesus monkeys make the courting gesture of smacking their lips and making pleasure calls when they get a PEA cocktail (Fisher 1992).

While these chemicals are great for getting mammals together for bonding and the reproduction that often follows, it isn't the *sign of the soul mate* that we humans take it to mean. An infatuation period can be important to the long-term well-being of a marriage if the players don't mistake it for mature love. It can be good for marriage because it provides a positive memory to draw upon when, inevitably, the going gets rough. With early romance, there is the experience that finally we're going to be loved in the way we want and deserve to be. It may be the only opportunity, other than childhood, where we get to experience some version of unconditional love, because both parties are working so hard to make the other happy.

However, the heady phase of newfound romance doesn't last, and that's often a disappointment, no matter how seasoned we are in relationships. It's disheartening because it means that we have to either break up or start dealing with our expectations of what a real relationship is going to be like with this person. This means moving into the uncomfortable realm of facing the imperfections of our partner and ourselves.

In *Anatomy of Love: A Natural History of Monogamy, Adultery and Divorce,* anthropologist Helen Fisher observes that cultures around the world recognize both the infatuation stage of romance and its natural end. She cites a study of 168 societies, which found that 87 percent of these different cultures evidenced an awareness of the rise and fall of the "falling in love" phase (Fisher 1992). Nisa, a

!Kung woman of the Kalahari Desert, described it in the following way: "When two people are first together, their hearts are on fire and their passion is very great. After a while, the fire cools and that's how it stays" (Shostak 1981, in Fisher 1992).

Surprisingly, few of these realities of marriage have filtered down into the American culture. For example, in the past thirty years there has been a huge increase in popular awareness of how to be a good parent. This stems from educational, economic, and cultural changes that emphasize the child's need for love, empathy, and reflection. In the same time frame, there has been a growing body of research on what makes marriage work and what is reasonable to expect from it.

However, unlike with parenting practices, many people still believe that marriage should be a continuous wellspring of happiness, and panic when the inevitable cooling-off period begins. Highly educated people come into my office every day with the same script of marriage that is being recited by the actors in the romantic movie at the cineplex down the street. Their expectations of themselves, their spouses, and their marriages have little to do with what is reasonable to expect from a long-term relationship. They carry a Hollywood and Madison Avenue version of love and an ideal of contentment that have everything to do with selling popcorn and nothing to do with long-term happiness.

A study that compared the attitudes of college students in the 1960s and 1990s found that students now have higher expectations that marriage will meet their needs for companionship, personality development, and emotional security.[5] Another study found that the percentage of couples describing their marriage as "very happy" declined between 1973 and 1988 (Glenn 1991, in Amato and Booth 1997). If marriage is now defined as a place to satisfy emotional needs, then people may be more likely to abandon relationships that don't promote personal growth in spite of the many other advantages to marriage such as successfully raising children, companionship, and increased financial security (Amato and Booth 1997).

Individual expectations are often unconscious and result from our relationship to important caregivers. If you felt loved, admired, and appreciated as a child, you are more likely to expect this in your own marriage. Conversely, if you were abused, neglected, unappreciated, or devalued, you are more vulnerable to repeating this pattern in your marriage, with unconscious beliefs that dissatisfaction, neglect, or abuse are basic facts of life that should exist unchallenged. You may also perceive these qualities in your marriage when they don't exist.

Paula: I grew up as a child thinking that every household was as sorry as mine. My parents couldn't stand each other and didn't seem to be too crazy about me or my brother, either. A lot of my friends' houses were like that, too, so I don't think I made too much of it. When I got married, I didn't have the highest hopes in the world. I figured you just knuckled under the way Mom and Dad did and were grateful for what you got.

We all bring the unmet needs from childhood and our past into our marriages. If we were rejected, we're dying to be loved; if we were smothered, we're struggling to be independent; if we were criticized, we're praying to be admired; if we were neglected, we're desperate to be seen. These feelings persist in a constant state beneath our deceptive exteriors and influence our aspirations, our dreams, and whom we choose as mates. When these needs are met in marriage, closeness and commitment often follow. When these needs are denied, feelings of betrayal, depression, loneliness, and rage can result.

Our expectations have to be tempered by understanding what's reasonable to expect from any marriage. In addition, we have to evaluate our expectations on the basis of whom we have chosen as partners. Part of my goal is to give you tools to determine whether you should keep pushing for change, stay and accept it for what it is, or get out. This means getting really clear on whom you married and what expectations, problems, and conflicts *you* bring to the party.

Several authors have attempted to categorize some of these irrational expectations. In *The Mirages of Marriage,* psychologists William Lederer and Don Jackson list numerous false assumptions, including the expectation that marriage is a cure for loneliness, or that arguing is a sign that your marriage is in trouble. Psychologist Janis Abraham Spring compiled a long list of irrational expectations in her book, *After the Affair.* Some examples are:

"My partner and I should feel a deep, unspoken bond at all times."

"My partner should be able to anticipate my needs."

"I shouldn't have to work for love."

"The chemistry is either right or wrong."

"My partner should be emotionally available to me whenever I need him or her."

"Love is a feeling that can't be forced or manufactured. It either exists or it doesn't."

"We shouldn't have to work at feeling sexual desire for each other; it should come naturally or not at all."

"When passion dies, so does the relationship."

True marital satisfaction is often guided by the principle found in the AA Prayer, "God grant me the ability to change the things I can, accept the things I can't, and the wisdom to know the difference." Marital researcher John Gottman notes that there are unsolvable problems in every marriage. Most often, the issue isn't the presence of problems, but how you interpret them and what you do about them. "Problems are inevitably part of a relationship, much the way chronic physical ailments are inevitable as you get older. They are like a trick knee, a bad back, an irritable bowel, or tennis elbow. We may not love these problems, but we are able to cope with them, to avoid situations that worsen them, and to develop strategies and routines that help us deal with them." He notes that marriages often get bogged down in "if onlies." "If only your spouse were taller, richer, smarter, neater, or sexier, all of your problems would vanish. As long as this attitude prevails, conflicts will be very difficult to resolve" (Gottman 1994).

University of Chicago sociologist Linda Waite and coresearchers found that a majority of unhappy couples with children were much more content with their marriages when polled five years later. Couples who stayed together were characterized by either a "marital endurance ethic," a "marital work ethic," or a "personal happiness ethic." In the marital endurance ethic, marriages improved, not because the partners fixed the problems, but because they outlasted them. Thus, problems with children, money, job changes, even infidelity healed through the passage of time. In the marital work ethic, members of the couple actively worked to solve the problems in the marriage through personal growth, behavior change, and communication. Some common strategies listed were arranging dates and time together; enlisting help from in-laws, therapists, or clergy; and threatening divorce and consulting with divorce attorneys. In the personal happiness ethic, the members accepted the limitations of the marriage and worked to find happiness outside of it (Waite 2000; 2002). Waite's study gives credence to the notion that, often, there are ways to stay married and achieve happiness, with or without your partner's help.

PERFECT PARTNERS

MANY OF THE individuals and couples I see are burdened with myths about what they're entitled to in marriage. If you believe what you see on television or in magazines, your spouse should be a confidant(e), aerobics partner, hot sex partner, mentor, financial planner, and part-time psychologist. Your partner should be empathic but not weak, assertive but not aggressive, warm but not dependent, independent but not distant. While some of these are useful, even important, the composite is hardly a requirement of a decent marriage.

As a rule, expecting to find happiness in marriage is a bad idea. This isn't to say that there is no value to marital compatibility or that a good marriage is incapable of contributing to your happiness. It's just that if you're not happy in the rest of your life, the probability of finding it in the hectic, stressful world of the modern marriage with children is quite low. In addition, looking for happiness in any cluster of personality traits in a partner assumes that our own needs are constant and stable. It assumes that, like a romantic dinner, we're being fed something by our spouses while we remain in the same state, moment to moment.

What attracts us can also repel us (Beck 1988; Spring 1997). We may feel soothed by someone's warmth and attention in the morning and feel smothered by it later as we're trying to get out the door. We may feel freed to be independent by a mate's autonomy and then experience him or her as aloof and uncaring the next day. We can feel drawn to his or her energy and vitality at one moment and experience this same behavior as self-involved and distracting when we're wanting to sit in silence and collect our thoughts.

Sometimes people choose someone who is the opposite of the person with whom they were last involved. In the beginning, this results in a dizzying excitement as the new partner begins to gratify the needs that were long neglected in the last relationship. Unfortunately, every positive trait has its downside as well. One of my clients put it this way; "I couldn't stand how dependent my first wife was. I felt like she wanted me to be her dad or something. Then, when I met Sylvia, she was so independent and strong. I felt like, 'Finally, a woman I don't have to take care of!' I felt like I could breathe again. But five years into it, I almost feel like Sylvia's *too* independent. I really liked it in the beginning, but now I feel like it's a problem because she won't let me get close to her."

THE ARRIVAL OF KIDS

THERE ARE TIMES in all marriages where it can feel pretty damned hopeless. One of the most predictable times is when children come on the scene. Numerous researchers have shown that a majority of marriages become significantly worse after children (Belsky and Pensky 1988; Belsky and Kelly 1999; Cowan and Cowan 1992; Gottman 1994). This is because there's a sudden diversion of emotional and financial resources away from the couple and into the kids. In addition, there is far less time to develop romance or think about a spouse's happiness. There is also less time and money to recharge or feel nurtured through hobbies, relaxation, or that hard-to-quantify "downtime." Heck, there's far less time to do almost anything when children first arrive.

> Sharla: Having kids was one of the turning points for our marriage, and not for the better. I think we were used to all of this time to hang out, relax, give each other back rubs, whatever. All of a sudden there's this nonstop crying baby on the scene and we were both caught unprepared for how it was going to affect our marriage. Before the baby, we were feeling like "This is going to be so good for the marriage," only it hasn't been. We're still trying to put it back together.

Marriages are often vulnerable to divorce or affairs at this time because there is a demand for each partner to grow and adapt to this new situation. Mates who seemed loving and devoted may look quite different from how they looked before kids. A husband who was selfless and involved with his partner before children may find himself irritable and unavailable after the kids arrive. A wife who was relaxed and easygoing may become anxious once she has the responsibility for and care of children in front of her. Children require us to be selfless in ways we may never have experienced before. Like marriage, parenting may tap our own unmet longings to be completely cared for and stimulate memories of all the ways in which we weren't. This may cause us to transfer the sadness, disappointment, and anger we felt in childhood onto a marital partner who is wrongly assigned the role of healing that wound.

Like many aspects of marriage, the arrival of children is often experienced differently by men and women. Many women experience having children as one of the more meaningful events of their lives (Person 1988; Belsky and Kelly 1994). For others, childbirth can represent an important, though sometimes confusing, stage of womanhood. As Crittenden (2001) writes, "With the arrival of a child, a mother's definition of accomplishment becomes more complex, her work load goes up, and her income and independence go down."

Conversely, many husbands feel displaced by this new person in the bed (or at the breast). They may feel jealous about their wife's new love object and resent her decrease in sexual desire. It is a commonplace that couples begin to have problems because sexual satisfaction is closely linked to marital happiness for husbands but less closely linked for wives, especially after the birth of the first child.[6] Thus, it's easy for husbands to begin to feel rejected or devalued at this point and for wives to feel sad or resentful that their partners aren't as involved or interested in the parenting experience.

While there's a great deal of variation with gender differences, women are more likely to reinvest this decrease in marital intimacy into increased caring for the child. They may resist getting a baby-sitter or doing activities that kept the marriage strong before kids arrived. Conversely, men may find themselves working later or suddenly becoming more interested in reclaiming long-lost interests. They may feel that the biggest contribution they can now make to the family is as a provider rather than as an involved parent (Belsky and Kelly 1994; Pruett 2000).

Gender can be a reliable predictor of divorce. Men who are belligerent, unaffectionate, or withdrawn are more likely to generate divorce fantasies in a woman, while women who are contemptuous, nagging, or aggressive stimulate thoughts of divorce in a man (Hetherington 2002). About one-third of divorces occur within the first four years of marriage (Kiecolt-Glaser and Newton 2001). Family researcher E. Mavis Hetherington writes in *For Better or Worse,* "For most couples, in the first four years of marriage as romantic love fades, marital satisfaction declines, then levels out, and then declines again in the seventh and eighth years as the seven-year itch arises. It never fully recovers again until middle age when for many couples there is a surge in marital happiness as the children leave" (Hetherington and Kelly 2002).

STRESS AND CRISIS

IF WE LIVE with someone long enough, marriage will be disrupted by some kind of stress or crisis: a job loss or some other serious conflict surrounding finances, a serious illness, or the death or disability of a parent. We may get affected by intrusive in-laws, meddlesome or divisive friends, a diagnosis of infertility, or problems with depression, anxiety, drug addiction, or alcoholism. Any of these stressors can turn a potentially decent marriage into a troubled one. This is because a crisis for one member of a family is almost always a crisis for the others. Your view and expectations of these stressors greatly affects how you handle them.

For some couples, marriage gets easier as there is a decrease in the trials and workload of children or other life stresses. However, that's not true for everyone. Many marriages get gridlocked and, without intervention, never recover. Their problems compound as they begin a downward spiral of anger, withdrawal, blame, or alienation. If this goes on for years, it can wear away any reservoir of good feelings that were in the marriage prior to the children or crisis. Developing strategies to either revitalize your marriage or accept what can't be changed is crucial to your happiness and the happiness of those around you.

CONCLUSION

EVERYWHERE WE LOOK, we're told what we're entitled to have in life and in marriage. Just about every commercial begins or ends by telling us what we deserve, from hamburger houses to diamond dealers to credit-card hawkers. However, neither marriage nor happiness has a lot to do with being a good consumer. Happiness isn't a product you can buy, nor can it be found by solving the problems in your partner's personality. These myths may account for why Americans, who have such a high standard of living and consume self-help literature at record rates, also have such a high rate of depression.[7] Unhappiness in marriage often occurs when we fail to grieve for what we're not going to get from our partners. This is where we turn next.

2

The Hoped-For Marriage

Learning to let go

"I've never had the marriage I thought I'd have and that's been hard for me to accept. Everywhere I go, people are holding hands, taking romantic vacations, having sex (at least I assume they are), and riding around in their convertibles telling each other the kind of funny, intimate things that couples say who ride around in convertibles telling each other funny, intimate things. I guess I've concluded that the man of my dreams will be remaining there because he won't be sharing my bed anytime in the near future. At least not while I'm awake!"
                                                    —BARB, AGE THIRTY-THREE

I HEAR PEOPLE struggling with some version of this issue every day in my practice. Some had a decent marriage before children, but haven't got their marriage back on track. Others have never had intimacy, romance, or fulfilling sex in their marriage, yet they successfully raised their children and peacefully coexisted in the same house for years. Some have so much contempt and hatred for each other that it's surprising they haven't killed each other . . . yet.

The problems in your marriage may be a function of irrational expectations, stress, or other issues. However, it may be that you're married to somebody who's really difficult for you. Or that you, in some important way, have outgrown your partner, and the relationship hasn't changed enough to accommodate this growth. As anthropologist Mary Catherine Bateson writes, "The people we live with are in many ways strangers, changing as fast as we get to know them. The problem in our era is that spouses become more youthful, stronger, or smarter, suddenly develop new talents and new aspirations or assert new needs. What do you do when a spouse or partner, rather than preferring someone new, seems to become someone new? It used to be common to urge young couples to wait and really get to know each other; now they may wait for five years without tying the knot, and lo and behold, they still discover they don't know each other" (Bateson 2001).

An example of outgrowing a partner is when both members of a couple are alcoholics and one of the members gets into recovery and the other refuses to. Another example is someone who marries out of desperation, or makes a poor choice because of low self-esteem. As her self-esteem improves or she becomes less desperate, she realizes that she made a choice that she might not have under better circumstances. This is likely part of the reason that people who marry young are the most vulnerable to divorce (Amato and Booth 1997). When we have children, we make decisions that affect the rest of our lives from a vantage point quite different from where we'll be decades later.

We don't always know what's going to be revealed to us about ourselves or our partners over time. You or your partner may be gay or lesbian and realized it later in the marriage, or married during a time or place where gay parenting was more forbidden.

In any event, whether it's accepting differences or disappointments, or learning how to live with a truly difficult spouse, your serenity will depend on your ability to grieve for what you're not getting and may never get from your marriage. Grieving may also help you to change a dynamic in the marriage that's harmful to you. For example, research shows that the majority of couples who divorce have marriages that are characterized by the "distancer/pursuer" dynamic (Hetherington 2002; Amato and Booth 1997). In this situation, a partner, usually the wife, continues to seek intimacy, contact, conversation, or reassurance from a husband who wants privacy and shuts down in response. Over time, the dynamic becomes painful for both because the pursuer becomes critical, nagging, complaining, and hostile while the distancer becomes cold, angry, and increasingly unavailable. If you're the pursuer, grieving that you're not going to get what you want from your partner may help you to end this problematic dynamic; if you're the distancer, grieving that you won't be able to get what you want through distance may help you behave in a less problematic fashion.

Letting go is an important step because it creates the opportunity to put your attention and energy into more productive ways to attain happiness and meaning. Failing to let go increases the likelihood that you'll continue to get hurt, disappointed, and angry by pursuing needs and desires that your partner may not be able to fulfill. This chapter begins with where you must begin, learning how to grieve for the loss of the marriage you thought you'd have.

LETTING GO

IN 1969, ELISABETH Kübler-Ross wrote her now famous book *Death and Dying*. While her work was not written on the topic of the present book, I have found her steps useful for helping individuals and couples examine the stages of letting go of the hoped-for marriage. This process involves coming to terms with your denial, anger, bargaining, and despair, and moving to acceptance.

DENIAL

Facing denial is the cornerstone of beginning to change your stance in your marriage. Denial can be hard to recognize because it's based on keeping one part of yourself hidden from another part. Denial has to be distinguished from a healthy feeling of hopefulness. With hope, there is the recognition that marriage takes work and commitment. Hope recognizes that what isn't working well today may work well later.

Marital change doesn't come in every marriage, however, even with time, commitment, and consistent effort. Hope becomes denial when you refuse to recognize that the person you've chosen is, now or forevermore, unable to change or provide you with the kind of love or involvement you seek. There are two forms of denial. In the first, you deny the limitations of your partner because it's too painful to accept those limitations.

> Becky: I spent the first ten years of marriage hoping that Bob was going to be different. I always wanted to be with a man who was more affectionate, but he's just not. I had a real "maybe, someday" type of mentality that I would tell myself when I'd start feeling depressed or hopeless. Once I gave up on getting that from him and just accepted it, I didn't feel so hurt and disappointed all the time. I also stopped nagging and criticizing him about how much he wasn't giving me.

In the second form of denial, you avoid seeing how your partner's behavior is hurtful to you or the kids.

> Sam: Regina yells a lot at the kids and I used to tell myself it wasn't a big deal. I grew up in a large Italian family and yelling was just a part of life. I wasn't facing that Regina's behavior was out of control in a way that my mother's never was. It wasn't until the school called us and told us they were worried about my daughter that I broke through my denial and realized that something had to change.

Statements of denial often begin with "It's not so bad," "He'll change," "If only I did . . . ," "If only I didn't . . ." In the short term, denial can be useful to protect you from painful feelings or situations over which you have no control. In the long term, it can cause you to ignore or tolerate behavior in yourself or your spouse that should be stopped.

People who are self-critical are sometimes the most vulnerable to denial. They are the least likely to recognize mistreatment and the most likely to feel undeserving of change. People who stay in relationships with abusers are the most poignant example of this. However, denial is much more common in marriage than most people realize. Many subtly sell themselves and their partners short with low expectations, held in place by denial statements such as "This is as good as it gets," "I want too much," and "I'm not that hurt."

It's crucial to consider what feelings or actions you might be avoiding through your denial because understanding the ways that you use denial can be an important gateway to growth and happiness. You may be in denial because it helps you avoid taking action on behaviors that are scary or challenging. Consider how you would complete the following: If I wasn't in denial . . .

- I'd demand that my partner change (get a job, get into therapy, get into recovery, be nicer to me).
- I'd demand that I change (go back to school; demand better treatment from my partner, children, or friends; get into recovery; get into therapy; take better care of my health).
- I'd be a lot more assertive.
- I'd get more support.
- I'd change my priorities.
- I'd have more fun.

ANGER

Anger can be a natural reaction to not getting what you want. It can be a signal that something is wrong and needs fixing, such as when you're being treated in a disrespectful way or are accepting less than you deserve in life. In a receptive or workable partner, it can be a useful tool to keep yourself aware of what's not working and orient you or your spouse toward addressing it. It can also be a useful first step to finding your voice when making the important journey from timidity to assertiveness.

However, anger can keep you helplessly tethered to a partner who is unable to meet your needs or is uninterested in meeting them. This is why the pursuer/distancer dynamic is such a strong predictor of divorce. In the stage of grieving, anger may be evidence you haven't accepted that you may not get what you want from your partner.

Constance: My husband always missed my birthday, and every year I would throw a fit. And it wasn't just birthdays; anniversaries, Valentine's Day, Christmas. I guess if he was a great husband in the other areas, I wouldn't mind so much, but I think this is just more evidence that he doesn't want to put a lot of effort into our marriage. So I made a decision that I'm going to stop getting mad about it, because the effort's not going to happen. He's not that kind of husband and I can't keep pretending. I find that I'm happier this way. I don't get disappointed, and the kids don't have to hear us have another big fight about it.

Feelings of hurt, sadness, shame, or rejection often underlie anger. Your anger is based, in part, on some hope that your partner will change. It's important to evaluate whether your partner *can* change or even *wants* to change. You may be avoiding the sad reality that your partner doesn't love you enough to care about your wishes. On the other hand, your angry disappointment may keep your partner so much on the defensive that he or she feels too criticized to want to behave differently.

This is an important decision point in your life, and you may need a therapist's help to make it. It's easy to fool yourself in both directions; that is, it's easy to fool yourself into feeling hopeful when you shouldn't, and it's easy to fool yourself into blaming your partner when you're just as responsible for perpetuating the downward cycle. Research shows that people in distressed marriages grossly underestimate how much their spouses are doing for them or for the family.[1]

If there's still reason for hope, you should spend your energy working on yourself and calmly working for change in your partner. However, if you have good evidence that it's unlikely that your partner will change, then you need to begin grieving that your marriage isn't going to be what you hoped it would be. Either way, it's important to gain control of your anger. Anger has the potential to poison your life and the lives of your children.[2] It can become so all-consuming that it takes time away from more productive activities. It may cause you to engage in self-destructive behaviors such as excessive use of alcohol, drugs, or food. Brooding about your marriage can create depression and make you less sensitive to your needs or the needs of your children.

BARGAINING

Bargaining is tied to denial. It is a trick your mind plays that goes: "I won't ask for this if I can have that." Through bargaining, an important part of you can get lost. It has to be distinguished from healthy compromising, where you learn that you often have to give something to gain something in marriage. With bargaining, you have sacrificed too big a part of yourself, only you pretend that it doesn't matter. This is a very important stage to understand and of which to gain control.

At the core of bargaining is a blind spot that often stems from your childhood. Somewhere you learned that you have to trade away important aspects of yourself to be loved. However, if you had to trade away important parts, only a false self was being loved; a "good child," a "smart child," an "independent child," an "unburdensome child." You needed to do this in your childhood to survive, but if you're doing it in marriage, you're losing a powerful opportunity to grow, change, and discover hidden resources in yourself.

Celine: I knew that if I made my mom feel like she was this fantastic person, then maybe I could get a scrap of attention. But it kinda twisted me because for the longest time I thought that was the deal with whoever I was with—you know, give 300 percent and get 5 percent back. My husband definitely benefited from that structure and he wasn't too happy when I started changing the rules, but he's dealing with it now because he has to. I'm not willing to play that game anymore. I'm a lot happier, that's for sure. I lost a few friends when I stopped being Mother Teresa, but I gained some better ones as a result.

Some common bargains in marriage are:

- I won't ask for what I want if you don't ask for what you want.
- I won't ask for what I want if you don't reject me.
- I won't talk about your issues if you don't explode.
- I won't be vulnerable if you don't withdraw.
- I won't make you work on your insecurities if you don't act wounded.
- I won't pursue my interests if you don't get upset.
- I won't be strong or successful if you don't get jealous.

The bargains you make say a lot about the areas in you that need strengthening for you to become happy, in or outside of your marriage. Some common examples where people need strengthening are:

- I need my spouse's approval to maintain my self-esteem.
- I'm too worried about people's needs and reactions.
- I don't believe I'm lovable as I am.
- I don't believe my needs are very important.
- I believe that other people are more important than I am.
- I am ruled by guilt, fear, or anxiety.

DESPAIR

Despair can be a sign that your marriage is bad for you. While I work hard in my practice to help people who want to stay married for the sake of their children, I don't believe that you should have to stay together if it makes you feel completely despairing about life. On the other hand, despair can be a natural part of the grieving process on the way to a healthier, more independent stance in your marriage. Despair is a common emotion that surfaces when you stop avoiding what you fear through anger, denial, and bargaining. Despair, in the stage of grieving, is the recognition that you are giving up something you really want. It is an important step to work through because in letting yourself face reality, you learn that you can survive and change.

> Hank: I felt really depressed when I finally realized that Shelley's self-centeredness may never change. I felt like, "I can't wait till the kids are in college. I have to get out of this marriage now!" But eventually I got through that stage. I still think she's selfish, but I've just come to accept that rather than feel like I can't be happy because of it. Would I stay married to her if we didn't have kids? Probably not. Do I want to put my kids or me through a divorce because of it? Definitely not. So now my attitude is more like, "Okay, she's selfish, so what?" Deal with it and stop acting like it's ruining my life.

Feelings of despair often have an irrational base. They are usually based on catastrophic thinking about yourself or negative forecasting about the future.[3] When people feel despairing about their marriages, it's not uncommonly a result of mentally circulating one or more of the following dysfunctional beliefs: If this is happening in my marriage . . .

- it means I'm unlovable.
- it means I'm a failure.
- I'll feel too lonely if it doesn't change.
- my life is over.
- I'll feel too empty.
- I'll feel too bitter.
- I'll do something drastic.
- I'll never be happy.

To reiterate, unremitting despair may be a message that your marriage is too painful for you to endure. On the other hand, it could be the bottom from which you push back more powerfully into reclaiming your life.

Acceptance

Acceptance is the final stage of letting go. It is a healthy recognition that your spouse deserves understanding and empathy. It means you have accepted that he or she isn't going to do what you want, and that doesn't mean you don't deserve to be loved or cared for. It also means accepting that if your partner can't or won't meet your needs, he or she is not a terrible person. Acceptance is crucial to finding happiness and represents the final stage to grieving the loss of the ideal marriage.

"Why should I accept my husband?" a client once demanded of me. "That jerk does nothing around the house and barely speaks to me. Why should I accept that?" You should absolutely spend time working to get your mate to change the behaviors that are important to you. This means that you communicate your needs and requests in a noncritical manner, strive to be assertive without being aggressive, eliminate your contempt, appreciate his or her strengths, examine your irrational expectations of marriage, and solve the problems that are solvable. If you are confident that you are in control of those behaviors, you consistently practice them, and your partner still hasn't changed, then you have to move toward accepting that this may be as good as it gets for now, and maybe forevermore.

It may take a long time to learn how to accept your spouse. Often, there are years of resentment, hurt, betrayal, and disappointment that contribute to feeling anything *but* acceptance! However, it is not in your best interest to devote all of your energy to hoping or waiting for change.

And acceptance doesn't mean you accept everything. Acceptance doesn't mean that you tolerate inappropriate behavior. For example, it doesn't mean being a doormat for your partner's problems or insecurities. It doesn't mean that you tolerate physical abuse, or mental cruelty toward you and/or your children. Acceptance doesn't mean that you like or admire his or her behavior all or most of the time, or that you adopt a martyred, passive, or soldierly state of mind.

Charlene: I grew up in a home where my father used to hit my mother, so it's no surprise that I ended up in the same kind of marriage. It wasn't until I got strong enough to stand up to Harold that I began to feel better about my life. I can accept a lot about him, and I have, but that's where I draw the line. He hits me or the kids, and I call the police, end of story.

Acceptance creates a more tolerant environment for your children
Children thrive in a household without judgment. It isn't enough for us to love our children if we're openly hating our spouses. This doesn't mean that you never have conflict with your mate. Children can tolerate parental conflict as long as they're not blamed for the conflict and if the conflicts get reasonably resolved.[4] However, it's also crucial that you manage your conflict in a way that is respectful of your children's need to respect and admire the other parent. If your mate is behaving in a way that isn't admirable, your children

will only be hurt by hearing your criticism or contempt. They will need to come to their own conclusions.

Acceptance shows your children that people can still be happy in life, even if they're not getting exactly what they want
This is an important lesson for our kids. If we pout, throw temper tantrums, shut down, or yell whenever a mate behaves in a way that we don't like, we're saying to our kids, "This is a reasonable way to respond to feelings. It is so intolerable for me to not have my needs met that I can't control myself." This is the last message you want to send. Our children use us as guides to know which feelings are okay to experience and express. They also count on us to show them how to tolerate feelings of disappointment, rejection, criticism, or withdrawal in a way that will be useful for them in their future relationships.

For example, part of the reason kids reject us during adolescence is because they need us to model healthy responses to rejection and devaluation. These feelings are common in the social domain of the teen, and there's no better way for them to learn how to handle rejection than to do to us what's being done to them and see how we handle it. (Lucky us.) Ideally, we tolerate their rejection and strive to walk the line between close friend and someone who's comfortable setting limits. If we consistently cave in to their rejection of us and become devastated, or irrationally critical or rejecting in response, we fail them by showing that people can't be emotionally detached in the face of getting rejected. If we can maintain our equanimity (or fake it until we call a friend), we're demonstrating that these feelings are manageable.

Similarly, while nobody likes feeling disappointed, hurt, or rejected in marriage, how we handle those feelings is crucial for our children. As psychologist Martin Seligman writes in *Learned Optimism*, "Being angry and fighting are not a human right. Consider swallowing anger, sacrificing pride, putting up with less than you deserve from your spouse. Fighting is a human choice, and it is your child's well-being, more than yours that may be at stake." While you may start out changing your behavior for your kids (a very good motivator), you will discover that, with practice, your feelings are more under your control than you previously realized.

Acceptance feels better than resentment and disappointment
It is impossible to have a happy life while simultaneously being consumed with hatred, hurt, or resentment. You can get control of the feelings that feel so out of control using the techniques and strategies described throughout this book. Chronic feelings of resentment and disappointment are toxic at the physical and emotional level, to you and your children.

> Marilyn: I used to have a fit about what a slob Dave was. A fit! It felt so disrespectful of me, and I didn't like him acting like I was his slave or something. I used to think that yelling at him about it was showing my daughter that you don't have to put up with it, but she'd always defend him, which just made me madder. I realized I was expending a huge amount of time and energy trying to get him to change and it was ruining my life. I wish I could say he's no longer a total slob but I can't. It's just that I changed how I think of him and it makes me feel better.

Acceptance makes your partner feel more understood, which increases the possibility that he or she will reciprocate in kind
If you can come to accept your partner, he will experience that acceptance, even if he doesn't say it or admit it. Few people change because there is a gun to their head, at least in any lasting way. Most people are motivated to change because they feel cared about or accepted for who they are (Hendrix 1988; Gottman 1994, 1999). Acceptance increases the likelihood that your mate will *want* to change because it removes the passive or active resistance that is

caused by criticism. Again, I am not advising you to accept abuse or mistreatment, but to work toward accepting the whole person so that you are in better control of what you and your kids are exposed to.

Acceptance increases the likelihood that you'll treat your spouse in a way that doesn't cause your kids to feel worried, guilty, responsible, or disloyal

Kids want their parents to be happy. It is very distracting to their young lives to have parents who are chronically burdened or resentful. This makes them waste their attention worrying about their parents rather than pursuing their own goals. There are several reasons why this is so important.

Children who witness chronic marital unhappiness feel obligated to choose sides between their parents.

> Marshall: My mother hated my dad and she made no secret of it. When he wasn't there, she would tell us what an ass she thought he was, and when he was there, she could barely contain her hostility. When we were young, we sided with her, I guess because she was the one we were around most of the time and she seemed so hell-bent on getting us to agree with her. When I was a teenager, I started seeing more of my father's side and started standing up for him. In hindsight, I shouldn't have been in the position of having to side with either one of them. My father should have been strong enough to fight his own battles, and my mother should have found some other way to deal with her feelings than to constantly tell us what a lousy husband my dad was.

Children worry about their parents if they seem chronically angry, depressed, or unfulfilled.[5]

Often, children will inhibit their own goals and happiness out of a concern that they're being selfish or leaving a parent behind. They may feel obligated to devote an inappropriate amount of psychological resources to reassuring the troubled parent in reality or play. They may avoid their developmental goals as a way to not further burden that parent, or be too removed if the parent appears unhappy or overwhelmed. As adults, they may feel "survivor guilt" about having a better marriage than their parents. This may cause them to sabotage potentially good relationships or choose difficult partners out of loyalty to their parents' difficult marriage (Weiss and Sampson 1986; Vogel 1994; Zeitlin 1991).

Laura: My mom was completely overwhelmed by my dad and my brothers. They were all these rowdy, loud, aggressive males, and she was this soft-spoken little woman who believed she needed to practically ask permission to breathe. I was the youngest and the only girl. I remember feeling like I had to be a total good girl in order not to give my mother one more thing to worry about. I basically modeled myself after her, which wasn't great, seeing how she was such a martyr. It's taken me years to stand up for myself or even feel like I have a right to take care of myself. It would have been better if my mom had cared enough for herself or me to be a better role model.

Children memorize the behavior of their parents, and this affects their choice of partner, how they conduct themselves in marriage, and how happy they can be as adults.

A child who watches one parent humiliate the other parent is in danger of either enacting the same behaviors when he or she gets married, or becoming passive in response to humiliation.

Bruce: My dad was never nice to my mom. He basically treated her like she was this worthless little being that was in the world to serve him. I hated him for it. It wasn't until I was on marriage number three that I figured out I had turned out just like him. I still hear his voice in my tone whenever I get pissed

35

off. I have had to do a lot of work on myself to be a better parent and husband than he was.

You can always leave your marriage if you feel too miserable. But if you're going to stay in your marriage for the sake of your children, then it's important to work on accepting your spouse for who he or she is.

EMPATHY

PART OF FINDING HAPPINESS in any marriage has to do with recognizing your separateness from your partner. If your self-esteem is dependent on your partner's opinion of you, then you won't see him as a separate person, with his own needs and conflicts. Instead, everything will be seen through the lens of whether his behavior reinforces your sense of well-being and security or threatens it. Empathy helps you develop the psychological musculature to separate from your partner and become less dependent on his or her reactions. Empathy is the ability to get inside your partner and know what he or she is feeling and why. It's an attempt to have compassion for your partner's decisions or emotions, even when you disagree with them.

Understanding why your partner behaves in the sometimes confusing or alienating way that he does can help you communicate in a way that is productive for you and for your children. If you deeply understand your partner's position, then you are better able to summarize his feelings in a way that lets him know he is not crazy to feel the way that he does. Validating and understanding your spouse's position can help de-escalate conflicts and move toward more creative resolutions of problems.

There can be little long-term acceptance or serenity without at least some empathy in a marriage. Acceptance says, "I know you can't or won't change your behavior and I'm not going to try to change you." Empathy says, "I know you can't or won't change because you feel too scared to open up, too angry to try, too worried to let go." Empathy is the emotional bridge that can allow more productive interactions to occur. In addition, it can help you detach from your partner's behavior. If you know why your mate behaves in the way that he does, then it is easier to not blame yourself for his reactions.

> Monica: I used to feel upset whenever Liam and I talked about money because he would get so controlling and critical around it. Even once things got easier for us financially, it seemed like he couldn't relax with it. I'm a responsible person, but I'd always walk away feeling like I must be this total flake spend-thrift or something. It would make me feel really bad about myself, and pissed at him. Then he got into therapy and started talking with me more about how poor his family was growing up and how freaked out he was that we'd end up that way. I started understanding that he would worry about money no matter who he was with, it wasn't me. He's still way more worried about it than I am, but I feel like I don't take it so personally when he starts getting freaked out about it. I just figure he's running some old tapes and I'm not gonna get caught up in that.

Empathy gives you the opportunity to tap into whatever caring or loving feelings exist for your partner.

> Jonathan: I've stopped yelling at my wife all the time. One day, after this huge fight where I went off on her and the kids were all upset, I found her crying in the bedroom. It's not new for her to cry, it's just that there was something about it that time that made me think, "What am I doing? Do I really want to be some guy that's always yelling at his wife and making her cry in front of his kids?" It just suddenly seemed mean and

stupid to me. I apologized to her, which is something I haven't done a lot of in our marriage. She does piss me off a lot, but I stopped the yelling and that feels good.

FINDING EMPATHY FOR YOUR SPOUSE

SPEND SOME TIME THINKING about your spouse's childhood.

- What kind of feelings do you imagine he/she had growing up?
- Do you think she felt loved, cared for, and protected?
- In what ways do you think he was hurt, abused, neglected, or shamed?
- What were some significant experiences she had that shaped her feelings about love and intimacy?
- What kind of experiences do you think he was hoping to gain from marriage that were missing in his family?
- What kind of defenses do you think she put in place as a way never to be hurt again? How are those still operating?
- What kind of things make him or her happy? Sad? Scared?

Use this information as a way to contact caring thoughts or feelings for your spouse. Try to put those feelings in the form of something you like or appreciate about him or her. For the next six weeks, tell your spouse something that you like or value about him, in front of your children and when you're alone together. Do this three or four times a week and pay attention to your reactions to saying or feeling those things. How do your children respond to your voicing caring feelings for the other parent? How does your partner respond?

This appreciation or empathy does not have to be a promise of greater intimacy to come. It could be a statement such as "I appreciate what a great parent you are," or "I'm sorry you have to work so hard," or "I'm sorry I got so mad at you yesterday. I know that wasn't fair." However, the major goal is to help you maintain contact with your feelings of empathy, not to gain a specific reaction from him or her.

It is worthwhile to strongly encourage your partner to work on the behaviors and goals that are the most important to you before you accept that this is as good as it gets. To achieve this, there may be a time when you insist that your partner get into individual therapy or go with you to couple's therapy. If you think you're heading for divorce court if he or she doesn't change, an ultimatum may be in order. Some people worry that their mates won't get anything out of therapy if they're dragged there or sent there under coercion. However, many people can still benefit, even when they are brought in kicking and screaming.

SELF-COMPASSION

UNHAPPINESS IN MARRIAGE has the potential to disrupt or destroy our belief in ourselves. If we feel blamed, avoided, shamed, rejected, or disappointed on a regular basis, our self-evaluation can suffer. Without appropriate self-compassion, we are vulnerable to doing desperate, self-destructive, and marriage-destructive acts to try to avoid this pain.

Self-compassion is at the core of healthy self-esteem and immunizes us against the rejections or disappointments in and outside of our marriages. It gives us the strength to look at our mistakes and understand why we made them. Many confuse self-compassion with vanity or "sitting on the pity pot." However, it's neither vain nor self-pitying. It's a recognition that any form of self-hatred is destructive to you, your children, and your marriage.

While it isn't true that you can't love anyone until you love yourself, you are a lot more vulnerable to being rejected, manipulated, and mistreated by your partner and your kids if you don't. You're more inclined to make decisions that are based on the avoidance of pain than you are to act in ways that are good for you and your children. Also, if you don't love yourself, you're more likely to defend yourself in ways that are harmful.

Many find that using positive self-statements are useful for developing self-compassion and for countering the pathogenic beliefs developed from childhood. Add your own items to this list and practice them on a daily basis:

I am a good person, even if my partner is unable to help me feel that way.

I am deserving of forgiveness even when I sometimes blow it with my kids or spouse.

I am deserving of love and respect.

I don't have to rely on my partner for my self-esteem.

The more I can appreciate and value myself, the more I will have to give to myself and my children.

CONCLUSION

FINDING HAPPINESS IN THE difficult marriage means grieving that your relationship isn't going to be what you thought it would be. Acceptance, empathy, and self-compassion are three of the most empowering behaviors you can learn. With acceptance, you allow yourself to see your partner's limitations and accept that he or she is incapable or unable to be whom you want. Empathy is empowering because it allows you to see, with the greatest degree of clarity, who your partner is. It also allows you to see how your own reactions can bring out the least desirable aspects of his or her behavior. Self-compassion is important because it provides the basis for maintaining your self-esteem, regardless of the feedback you're getting from your spouse. It also allows you to forgive yourself for your inevitable transgressions as a partner or parent.

Cultivating an attitude of acceptance is an act of integrity. It's saying to yourself that you get to choose how you will feel and what you will say; that the buck stops with you in terms of the cycle of blame, shame, and hurt. And no matter what else is going on, you are committed to being the kind of person your children can look up to and admire.

We often don't know whom we're getting in marriage, and neither does our spouse. As the wedding veil gathers dust in the closet, we emerge as we are, for better or for worse. It's easy to lose yourself in a marriage with children. Often, the key to finding ourselves doesn't involve looking to the future, but through examining the past. And this is where we turn next.

3

Messages from the Past

How your childhood can affect your marriage

FINDING HAPPINESS in the difficult marriage is a holistic endeavor. To achieve it, you have to work on your emotions and the beliefs and attitudes that govern those emotions. You have to change your behavior, and the belief system that governs your thoughts, feelings, and reactions. Finally, you have to reevaluate how much meaning you have in your life, apart from your marriage.

To make this change, it's important to understand how you were shaped by your childhood environment and how your parents or other significant people's vulnerabilities, limitations, and choices affected your view of yourself and of the world around you. Humans have a longer period of dependency on their parents than any other mammal. We begin paying close attention to our parents' responses straight out of the womb.[1] Because of this dependency, humans evolved a sophisticated emotional system that ensures that we stay connected to our caregivers. We believe what our parents say to us and how they behave toward us because, from nature's standpoint, our lives depend on it. Viewed another way, if we didn't have this system, we'd be more likely to wander off into danger or suffer parental neglect or mistreatment.

While other animals and insects communicate such critical information as the presence of danger, the location of food sources, expressions of territory, dominance, submission, or mating availability through sounds, grunts, vocalizations, chemicals, and dances, humans are probably unique in how much *error* we can pass along to our offspring. This is problematic, since children lack the intellectual or emotional base of experience to know whether their parents' messages are correct. Thus, a woman who was constantly told by her mother that men can't be trusted complied with this belief by constantly choosing men who couldn't be trusted or by provoking men to behave in an untrustworthy fashion. A man whose father said that women are weak found himself avoiding women who disproved his father's theory, or ridiculing his wife whenever she showed any vulnerability. A child who was told that she was stupid assumed that her parents were right, even though her teachers thought her brilliant.

BACK TO THE PAST

I PROMISE NOT TO PURSUE the same path that many marital self-help books travel, which is to say that you can have a happy marriage if only you work hard enough on your communication. While good communication is essential to any good relationship, it isn't always enough to make a relationship gratifying. I also promise not to say that if you can't make your marriage satisfying, you should leave. There are three facts that I accept without contradiction:

1. You may be married to someone who, for whatever reason, has little capacity to be a fulfilling partner for you.

2. There are many worthwhile reasons to stay in a marriage with children, even when the person you're married to is difficult or unrewarding.

3. Being married to someone who is difficult or unrewarding need not ruin your capacity to have a happy life.

I will go into great detail about how to live with a difficult partner, or in an unrewarding marriage, throughout the book. However, it just may be that, as hopeless, and sad, and resentful, and trapped as you feel right now, you *may* feel better about your marriage at a later time. It is possible that you will see aspects of yourself in the following examples or exercises that allow you to experiment with a different way of being, and that this small experiment, consistently applied, will let some sunlight into that suffocating basement where you've been spending so much time. You may discover that small changes can breathe new life into a very tired relationship.

Anyway, even if it is all your partner's fault, you still have to develop yourself as a person to be happy. The place that you're stuck in your marriage can tell you a lot about where you're stuck in other areas of your life. And that's the beauty of marriage: it mirrors us like almost no other instrument of reflection, even when what it reveals is unappealing. This chapter is written to help you begin that process by looking at how your past affects what you bring to your marriage.

To do this, you'll have to be able to answer some tough questions about yourself:

- How much of your dissatisfaction with your partner is dissatisfaction with yourself?
- How are you unconsciously creating or contributing to the very problems you wish to solve in your marriage?
- To what extent are your experiences from childhood affecting your present experience of yourself and/or your partner?
- How many of your criticisms of your partner are aspects that you unconsciously aspire to, yet forbid yourself to have?
- In what ways are you overly dependent on validation and reassurance from your partner?
- How much do you look to your marriage as a source of fulfillment, while you neglect other important areas of your life?

My experience as a psychologist has led me to believe that most people's childhoods were more complicated than they remember or realize. If you have never had therapy, it's quite possible that your view of your past is somewhat idealized. One of the chief functions of the mind is to keep distracting and painful stimuli out of awareness. Among other things, seeing your childhood as better than it was allows you to attend to the present without being distracted by the past. It also allows you to preserve relationships with living parents or family members that might be more complicated by memories of their failings.

I'm not trying to convince you that you had an unhappy childhood—obviously, not everyone does. It's just as important to remember what was good in your past because that awareness contributes to a sense of strength and enjoyment of life. However, if you *are* avoiding memories and perceptions, you're paying a high price for it. In exchange for a more palatable view of childhood, you may be unconsciously blaming yourself for things that went wrong and projecting onto your partner inaccurate feelings and intentions. You may be vulnerable to playing out in your marriage and parenting the ways that you were hurt or affected by your family. If so, you may be compromising your own aspirations and potential.

CORE CONFLICTS

ON THE PULPIT of every self-help ministry there is the same sermon: "The only person you have any control over is yourself." The more you know about who you are and what drives you, the more you'll be on the road to making the changes in your life that create happiness and meaning. Personality, emotions, and attitudes are influenced by your genes and by the experiences you had in the family in which you grew up. Genetics can influence whether your temperament tends more toward the aggressive or the passive, whether you're outgoing or shy, sensitive or invulnerable, anxious or fearless, emotional or unemotional (Reiss 1995; Ploman et al. 1994; Pinker 2002). While these traits are hardly etched in stone, they nonetheless exert an influence on your personality, strengths, and vulnerabilities.

Our experiences with our parents help determine what we do with those strengths and vulnerabilities. Taking a small human and making it competent for the challenging world of marriage is no small feat. Heck, making it ready for college is a momentous achievement. For children to become competent adults and relationship dwellers, they need to have a number of important experiences, one of which is having their parents provide a good reflection of who they are. They should also learn what is and isn't reasonable to expect from others and be raised in a secure and predictable environment. They should learn how to depend on others and know how to be independent of another's control or influence. They should have an ongoing set of experiences during childhood and adolescence that contribute to and develop their self-esteem. They should learn how to be in touch with their feelings and learn how to communicate those feelings. If any of these needs aren't met when we're children, we may have to work harder in our marriages to find and maintain our bearings. We have to learn for the first time, and sometimes from the most unwilling tutor, how to communicate what we want and need, and what we can or can't get from another person.

Young children love their parents with as much force for their flaws as for their strengths because children can't discern them. Childhood love is beautiful to behold in part because it isn't capable of pausing. That's a skill that we develop only as we begin to be more separate. Children have only a few options for how to respond to their parents' messages; they can *comply, identify,* or *rebel.*[2] Children who comply behave as though their parents' treatment of them is correct and justified. For example, a child who is told that he is bad complies by experiencing himself as a bad child, and behaving in a way that others would label in that direction; in marriage, he might behave in ways that his partner would find troubling. Similarly, a child who is neglected complies by feeling unimportant and neglecting herself. In marriage, she might have a hard time being responsible, taking care of herself, or feeling important enough to assert her rights.

Children who identify use their parents' behavior as a model of how to behave. Thus, a boy who grows up watching his father treat his mother in a disrespectful way identifies with this behavior and treats his wife in a disrespectful way when he grows up. Or he might identify with a parent's passivity by having a hard time taking initiative as a child. As an adult, he might become overly passive in his marriage, much as his mother was in hers.

Children who rebel fight against the parents' treatment of them by behaving in opposition to the parents' treatment or wishes. Thus, a girl who grows up with parents who are moralistic and perfectionistic might struggle against this with delinquency or underachievement. A boy who is raised by parents who are worried and possessive may rebel against this by becoming excessively risk-taking. In marriage, he may feel overly restricted by reasonable requests of commitment or responsibility, and aggressively accuse his wife of trying to control him.

The choice of defense is likely a combination of inherited temperament and an unconscious assessment of how to best maintain a connection with the parent. For example, a child who is born with an aggressive temperament would be more likely to respond to an abusive parent by either fighting against that abuse (rebelling against the parent) or identifying with the parent's abusive behavior (becoming abusive to peers, siblings, or even parents). He would be less likely to comply by becoming passive and withdrawn in the face of it. Conversely, a child who is born with a temperament that tends toward shyness and avoidance would be more likely to comply with the parent's mistreatment. Thus, in the same family, this child would respond to the same parental abuse by becoming more withdrawn, or by engaging in self-abusive behaviors.

Parents may consciously and unconsciously influence whether their children use compliance, identification, or rebellion. Thus, an abusive father may reward a son's aggressiveness and punish it in his daughter. Similarly a depressed parent might reward a child for internalizing emotions because the parent doesn't have the energy to manage more energetic behavior. Thus, children might get rewarded or praised for being withdrawn or not showing any emotion, and punished for being lively, animated, or having a normal range of feelings.

In this chapter, I'll go over some of the common ways that childhood can affect behavior in marriage. Perhaps you'll recognize your own parenting, childhood, or spouse. The purpose of this section is to help you become aware of how the behavior of your parents influences you today. How we're loved or cared for as children can affect whom we choose as partners. There is no statute of limitations on the influence of our childhoods. They persist in affecting us until we die unless they have been excavated and sifted through. However, once this excavation has been achieved, there is the opportunity to build a new foundation with a stronger house for you and your children to live in.

Into the Mirror: The Impact of Having Parents Who Were Depressed or Neglectful

A child's sense of self is built upon a second-to-second, minute-to-minute, day-to-day mirroring process. It's through the process of mirroring that a self develops out of infancy. Parents who are chronically depressed, self-involved, or emotionally unavailable can do great harm to a child's developing sense of worth and identity because the parent is so out of sync with the needs and communication of the child (Brown et al. 1990; Seligman et al. 1984; Weissman, Warner, and Wickmarante 1997).

Thus, if your mother or father was constantly distracted when you were laughing, sad when you were happy, hurt when you were ecstatically lost in your own pleasure, or bored when you were mastering an important task, you likely concluded that there's something not very interesting or worthwhile about you. You may carry this confusion about yourself into your marriage, where it taints your ability to love and to receive love. Without adequate mirroring, a child's sense of self gets muted; it's like trying to discover what you look like from a mirror covered with gauze. As psychiatrists Thomas Lewis, Fari Amini, and Richard Lannon write in *A General Theory of Love,* "People differ in their proficiency at tracing the outlines of another self, and thus their ability to love also varies. A child's early experience teaches this skill in direct proportion to his parent's ability to know *him.*"

If your parent was depressed or neglectful, there might have been a reversal of roles. Rather than having the experience of being taken care of, you may have had to take care of your parent. Because children feel sorry for depressed and needy parents, they may be unaware of what they missed in their parents' unavailability. If your parent was depressed, you may sense something's wrong with you, but you don't know what. You can't understand why you have a hard time finding satisfaction in your life or in your relationships. You don't understand why you continually get involved in friendships and marriages where you give so much more than you get back or feel so unfulfilled by what you receive.

However, not all people with depressed parents look upon their childhood as deprived (Young and Klosko 1994; Young 1999). Sometimes a strong relationship between parent and child allows the child to get self-esteem by caring for the parent. To further complicate the picture, some parents show deep gratitude for that care, which can deepen the child's feelings of connection and loyalty to the parent. Finally, children who are *parentified* like this often develop genuine skills that can be useful in some ways, however compromising those skills may be in their marriage. They can become gifted listeners and caretakers, excellent at assuming responsibility. However, they are sometimes so confused by guilt and overresponsibility that they believe it's wrong to receive anything in return.

> Pete: I took care of my mother and I was glad to do it. I felt sorry for her. My father took off before I was born and she married this asshole who never took her anywhere or did anything for her. I felt like, "Hey, if I can bring some sunshine into the life of this woman who brought me into this world, then what's the problem with that?" Yeah, I didn't go to school dances and crap like that because it was all so stupid. I wasn't a mama's boy, but if it meant that I stayed home on Saturday night so mom had a little company, I don't see what the problem is in that.

While it's easy to understand Pete's feelings, the problem is that as an adult, he was ridden with guilt and excessive worry over others' feelings. In his marriage, he couldn't ask for anything from his wife for fear of burdening her. He excelled at caretaking and failed at understanding what he needed or knowing how to take it when it was offered. As a result, his marriage was weighed down by his resentment of his wife for not guessing his needs, because he felt too guilty and undeserving to voice them.

While a depressed parent can sometimes bond with her child, she is equally likely to make a child feel neglected because she is too tired or overwhelmed to attend.

> Yoni: I was the eldest of three girls and had a lot of responsibility growing up. My mom had a pretty serious depression; they tried everything on her and nothing seemed to work. Most of my childhood memories are of her sleeping on the couch or holed up in her room with the TV on. It was hard to get Mom to smile about anything. "Hey, Mom, I got straight A's! Hey, Mom, I got elected the class president. Hey, Mom, I got a scholarship."

Whatever it was, she'd just give her same "That's nice, honey" response and keep watching whatever show she had on. I remember feeling like I must be the most uninteresting person in the world.

In Yoni's marriage she was passive and withdrawn. She described feeling invisible to her husband. As a result, she felt lonely and unloved in her marriage and frequently fantasized about being with someone who would adore her. While her husband seemed willing to connect more with her, her own difficulties knowing how to connect caused her to reject him.

The effect on marriage

If you grew up with depressed or neglectful parents, you may seek an inappropriate amount of attention and stimulation from your partner to make up for how lost or empty you feel.[3] You may be drawn to the excitement of an affair because your inner world feels so lifeless. You might not have been able to rely on your parents, and this might have left you afraid of your normal desires to depend on your partner. This may also cause you to criticize your spouse as needy and dependent when he/she wants to be close to you in a reasonable way. You may feel drained by being a spouse and parent because you don't feel as if you have anything to draw upon.

On the other hand, if your parents were depressed, you may be vulnerable to giving more than you get from your spouse. In this case, you unconsciously comply with a belief developed in childhood that your role is to give to others, even if they give little or nothing to you. You may have married someone who is selfish because you don't know what is unreasonable for someone to ask of you. This may also cause you to be confused about setting appropriate limits and prioritizing your own needs for care. However, because you feel so deprived, you may wrongly view your partner's healthy attempts to be self-interested as selfish.

In the next section, and the sections following, I make recommendations for how to begin to address the issues raised in this chapter. These will be developed and elaborated throughout the book.

Path for change

- Reduce your dependency on your partner to make you feel worthwhile and alive. If you're too independent of your partner, work on letting him or her get close to you and be a more loving force in your life, if he or she is capable.
- Strive to take control of your life. Make plans for the future and carry them out. This will help you to reparent yourself and help you experience that the world is more interested in you than were your depressed or unavailable parents.
- If you're overly responsible, work on being less responsible for others. Learn how to tolerate and rechannel the anxiety and guilt you feel when you are doing things for yourself or when others are in need. You can begin to do this by starting to prioritize your own needs so that you are not at the bottom of the list. Use these pleasurable experiences to develop and enliven your inner world. Let others take responsibility and let them face the consequences when they have problems. Examine whether you give yourself power by letting your partner be weak.
- Use self-talk (chapter 8) to counter the self-criticism that stems from your guilt and overresponsibility.
- Work to understand how your childhood affected your attitudes about marriage. Consider with which parent you're more identified. Your feelings of depression, guilt, or worry may make it hard for you to be appropriately aware of how your parent's behavior affected you. The goal isn't to blame your parent, but to develop your understanding of what you needed.

Limits and Deservedness: The Impact of Having Narcissistic or Overindulgent Parents

A healthy sense of deservedness is good for marriage because it frees us to communicate our needs and to develop our feelings of pleasure and meaning. A sense of overentitlement is harmful in marriage because it leaves the other feeling burdened, resentful, and unappreciated. Children can be damaged by excessively entitled parents because the parents' needs for mirroring, praise, and empathy get prioritized over the child's (Miller 1981). Self-centered parents may greatly attend to the child when the child enlarges the parent, and ignore him or her when the child is involved in ways that leave the parent out. They might act jealous or threatened by a child's beauty or talent. Children who grow up in this environment often develop the belief that it's dangerous to attend too much to their own needs if those needs are at variance with those of the people they love.

Rebecca: My father was a black hole of needing to be center stage. At the dinner table he'd usually have some story about how he met this important person and how brilliant they thought he was. He was an entertainment attorney, so there was never any shortage of interesting people he was involved with. If we were bored or distracted or actually wanted to talk about what was happening in our meaningless little lives he'd act completely insulted and storm away from the dinner table, sometimes when someone else in the family was right in the middle of a sentence. But if you did something that made him look like a good parent such as star in the school play or whatever, he'd be like, "Yep, that's my girl. Taught her everything she knows." My husband is a milder version of my dad. In the past year I'm seeing how much I put myself at the bottom of the barrel in our marriage, and it's made me resent him. Now I have to learn how to value myself as much as I do him and our kids, which, as obvious as it sounds, is foreign to me. It's like growing a new personality.

While Rebecca complied with her father's message that she was unimportant, many identify with a self-involved parent and behave in a self-centered and demanding way in their own marriages. Another kind of family environment that produces excessively entitled behavior is when parents fail to adequately set limits on their children. Parents who "spoil" children fail to prepare them for marriage.

Klaus: I didn't have to lift a finger in my house, growing up. Pretty much whatever I said went. I think it's because both of them never had anything growing up from either of their parents—everybody was so poor and freaked out from the war. Their big motto was "We don't want you to ever experience what we went through. We want you to have the life we never had." So I never really had to work to make things happen.

Klaus's attitude was a serious strain on his marriage because he never learned the concept of reciprocity. Even though his wife had a full-time career, he wanted her to wait on him when he got home and take full responsibility for the parenting. He acted bored when she would complain about her difficulties, though he insisted that she give him her undivided attention whenever he spoke. His marriage floundered because he took his wife for granted. People who are raised in an environment like Klaus's believe they're entitled to one-way giving. They are often unmotivated to change because they seem to be getting what they want, as they always have. It's often not until it's too late or until they're delivered an ultimatum that they consider changing.

A weak parent can produce children who are excessively entitled

Doug: Mom never got over her divorce from my dad and it was really pathetic. Even when I was a teenager she'd sit around crying, "I just don't understand why he left, I just don't understand it." I didn't really respect her, it's like, "Get over it, move on. He's gone and good riddance." If I wanted money or whatever I'd just bully her until I got what I wanted. She was really easy to intimidate.

Doug had problems in his marriage knowing how to share power with his wife. He had never developed the ability to accept influence from a woman and thus used the same bullying techniques in marriage that he had used on his mother.

An environment of deprivation can produce feelings of excessive entitlement

Nell: I grew up pretty poor in West Texas. My ma was a very worried, depressed, and dependent woman, and my dad might have uttered two words a year. Ma was in and out of the hospital all of the time for every illness you can think of, though I don't think they ever found a real problem. I was an only child and got a job at twelve so I could help support the family, but mostly so I could have an excuse not to be there. It was pretty suffocating, I guess the way they show mental institutions on TV with people sitting in the dark, never saying anything. They weren't bad people, they just didn't have a lot to give me. I felt like if I stayed there one more day I'd wind up like them with the life sucked out of me.

After high school Nell married a man who was quiet and withdrawn, much like her dad. However, she rebelled against her childhood environment of overresponsibility and deprivation by

55

becoming demanding and overly entitled in her marriage. Despite her husband's modest income, she racked up thousands of dollars of credit card debt buying expensive clothing for herself and expensive toys for the children. When he wanted to talk about a budget or suggested that she get a part-time job to pay down their debt, she became enraged and accused him of trying to deprive her of enjoying her life.

The effect on marriage

If you are identified with a narcissistic parent, or if you're complying with your parents' overindulgence of you, then you may have unrealistically high expectations of attention and care from your partner (though you probably wouldn't recognize this in yourself). You may possess unrealistic notions about the amount of work one has to do to maintain a marriage. You may have a hard time empathizing with those around you and feel superior to your spouse and others. You often express your feelings like an enraged child rather than a mature adult. You're the least likely to get help because you don't believe you have a problem.

On the other hand, it's possible that you comply with your parents' self-centeredness by feeling unimportant in your marriage and life. You may feel guilty about valuing your needs because you were raised to prioritize the needs of others. You may carry a feeling of emptiness because you were never given a sense that your own feelings and ideas matter. You may also have chosen a partner who is overly self-involved because you unconsciously comply with the belief that others' needs are more important than yours.

Path for change

- Examine your sense of entitlement and where it came from. Learn to see it as self-destructive, rather than a pathway to happiness. Develop a work ethic toward marriage that says you can't take out what you don't put in.

- If your partner accuses you of being selfish, consider the possibility that there may be a grain of truth to it.
- If you were overly indulged, you may have a hard time structuring your time, and may procrastinate or avoid as a way to force your partner into structuring your time for you. Thus, develop small goals for yourself both in and out of marriage and work to achieve them on a daily or monthly basis. Consider individual, group, or couple therapy to help you gain a more appropriate perspective on your contributions to the problems in your marriage.
- If you weren't helped to achieve independence, you will have to work hard to be an independent adult. You will need to challenge yourself and take risks in order to experience the rewards of independent behavior.

SECURITY AND PREDICTABILITY: THE IMPACT OF BEING RAISED IN A CHAOTIC OR THREATENING ENVIRONMENT

The childhood experiences of emotional security and predictability are the most basic building blocks of identity. Infants deprived of predictable and consistent human contact develop significant problems relating to others. John Bowlby observed that infants who feel the most secure are the most likely to feel comfortable exploring their environment (Bowlby 1953, 1972, Hrdy 1999). This need for security is apparently true for all mammals. Monkeys who are raised without a consistent parent do poorly in their social relations with other monkeys and attain low status within their group. They demonstrate lower levels of the neurotransmitter serotonin than those raised in a secure environment. These results have been found in many mammals (Lewis et. al 2000).

When children are raised in environments filled with chaos, threats, or abuse they bring considerable fears of abandonment and mistrust into their marriages. Children who grow up in these environments may also develop beliefs that they don't have the right to set limits on a spouse's hurtful behavior.

Andrea: My father molested me for six years, and when I finally told my mother about it she blamed me. It was enough of a nightmare having him come into my room whenever he was high, but then to have my mother side with him and not believe her own daughter, that was too much to even stomach. I dropped out of high school and proceeded to go from shitty relationship to shitty relationship after that and through two marriages. I just let men treat me the way my father did, like I was there to be used. By my third marriage, I've had to learn the hard way to stand up for myself. I've got a long long way to go on that one, but I'm at least on the road instead of lying in a ditch beside it.

Andrea internalized the destructive messages of her mistreatment. While it's not a hard-and-fast rule, women are more likely to internalize by blaming themselves when hurt, while men are more likely to blame others (Leibenluft 1998). As adults, people who internalize mistreatment become passive in the face of abuse and confused about whether they have a right to defend themselves. The "battered woman syndrome" (Walker 1984) is an example of this process of internalization.

Externalizers, conversely, respond to hurt or trauma by making the other person the victim. Their unconscious strategy is to be sure they're not in the position of vulnerability by being in complete control. Thus, a common pattern is that partners who are batterers come from homes where they were abused as children or witnessed a parent being abused.

Some avoid the memory of painful experiences by either failing to get involved with others, or only involving themselves with people who won't hurt them (Zeitlin 1991).

Brenda: I chose Sal because I knew he wouldn't hurt a fly and neither would I. He and I never raise our voices at each other and we're very supportive. We try never to disagree and I think that's been our strength.

While this *can* be a strength, marriages like this are vulnerable to disruption when there's a crisis or when one of the members grows enough to want to change the rules (Gottman 1994). In either case, it requires the ability to tolerate the anxiety of conflict, something that avoiders fear doing. If you were raised in an abusive environment, you may have developed your identity around being prepared for the worst. You likely either withdrew into a shell or became wild as a way to shout down your anxiety and fears. As you entered adolescence, you may have used drugs or alcohol as a way to manage your anxiety, fear, or upset (Black 1981). If not, you may have found other costly ways to withdraw or manage your fear and anxiety, such as bulimia, phobias, obsessiveness, or perfectionism.

Effect on marriage

You may misinterpret any criticism as an act of betrayal or war. This could be either out of an identification with a critical parent or as an effort to protect yourself. You may be vulnerable to having affairs or engaging in potentially self-destructive behaviors as an attempt to manage your fear of being left or hurt. You may often feel scared and alone and constantly wait for the ax to fall. You may blame your partner for your feelings of anxiety and vulnerability and insist that he or she demonstrate loyalty or devotion in ways that are neither reasonable nor possible. You may get your partner to reject you as a way of proving that your worst fears are true (and that your parents were right to mistreat you). You may be obsessed with maintaining control of yourself and those around you, such as your mate and children, or you may be married to someone who controls you.

Path for change

- Learn how to soothe yourself so that your anxiety is not such a dominant feature of your emotional landscape by using self-talk, affirmations, and relaxation techniques (see chapter 8).
- Don't tolerate abuse in your marriage or your friendships. If

you've been the abusive one, get help right away for your sake and the sake of your children, as we'll discuss in chapter 7.

- Decrease your spouse's potential to make you feel scared or intimidated, through assertiveness techniques and social support. If you're in an abusive marriage, you may have to leave or greatly change the structure of your marriage. Either way, you will need a supportive group of friends or family members to help you feel loved and safe in the world. Because you may be fearful of being hurt, it may be hard to reach out to others; however, it is critical to your happiness that you do so. There is no shortcut around this one.

- Learn that you are more resilient than you believe yourself to be. Your mind plays a trick on you, scaring you into believing you're on the edge of a thirty-foot drop when it's only three feet. You possess resources and defenses that you didn't have when you were a child; however, you can only discover this by taking risks. While it is sometimes painful when things don't go the way you want them to, it will not be the catastrophe that you're telling yourself.

- Learn to tolerate the anxiety that receiving help engenders. Stop waiting for others to call you or acting martyred when they don't.

- Develop a soothing set of beliefs to replace that sadomasochistic symphony that's constantly playing in your head. Some examples are "I am deserving of love and attention" and "If something happens, I have the resources to solve it."

- Learn that keeping your partner on the defensive by shouting or shaming is an illusory safeness. Take responsibility for the ways you push your partner away. Disengage from your spouse if either of you escalates the conflict.

- Write a letter to the people who have hurt you. You can decide later whether to send it or not. In the letter, tell them that they were wrong to abuse you when you were the most vulnerable. Let them know how you have suffered in life as a result of their neglect or abuse. Let yourself get angry, as it will help you fight against your internalized messages from them. It may also help you to place your anger where it belongs.

- Don't blame yourself. It wasn't your fault that you were abused.
- Make amends to people whom you have hurt in the past. Ask for forgiveness.

BOUNDARIES: THE IMPACT OF PARENTS WHO ARE OVERLY RESTRICTIVE OR CONTROLLING

Parents who are overly restrictive create children who feel crowded and controlled in relationships. As adults, they often respond to this experience by either becoming controlling, choosing a partner who is controlling, or wrongly viewing their partner's behavior as controlling.

Pam: My dad was a control freak and I hated him for it. I wasn't allowed to go to friends' houses after school like all the other kids because I had to be home, where he could keep an eye on me. It's like he thought I was on the verge of committing some crime all of the time, even though I was a really good kid. When I got into high school he turned the screws even tighter. I couldn't grow my hair out, I wasn't allowed to date because, of course, I'm going to go right out and get pregnant. I had to wear clothes that looked like something my grandmother would have worn. I basically wasn't allowed to have any say over any part of my life.

Pam's background caused her to be hypersensitive to any request for compromise from her husband. Her constant refrain with him was "You're not my father. You don't get to tell me what to do." She viewed him as trying to dominate and control her when he would want her to negotiate in the ways that are reasonable in marriage. Over the course of their relationship, her husband gradually withdrew from her into a cloud of resentment and frustration.

Parents are sometimes restrictive out of excessive worry

> Anthony: My mother was a major worrier and saw danger constantly lurking around the corner. If I was riding my bike outside and she saw me fall, she'd rush outside crying, "Are you all right? Are you all right?" It was so embarrassing. I remember being in the eighth grade and it started to storm, and I looked out my classroom window and was horrified to see mother running to the school carrying my boots, so I didn't "catch my death of cold," which, according to her, I was always on the verge of doing. But it was like that with everything. I couldn't do anything without her freaking out about it.

Anthony's experience made him very passive in his marriage. Like many people who aren't raised to be competent or take risks, he chose a wife who overfunctioned. This caused problems in his marriage because she resented him for not taking enough responsibility and he resented her for contributing to his feelings of incompetence.

Effect on marriage

If you felt overly controlled or restrained as a child, you may have developed an inappropriate need for independence as a way to fight against that experience. You may confuse reasonable nurturance or concern with worry and intrusion. You may have a hard time negotiating with your partner because you worry that you'll be dominated. However, this may make you controlling and domineering, much as a parent was with you.

If you are complying with your parents' treatment, you may have become excessively docile or dependent in life and marriage. You may have chosen a partner who controls and manages your life because you believe that you are unable to, or you believe that others need you to be in a submissive position. You may lie about small things in order to stay out of trouble with your mate or give yourself a feeling of independence.

Path for change

- Work on being independent and close at the same time. This means learning to tolerate the anxiety that comes when your partner needs you or wants to spend time with you. Learn that you can be giving and not lose yourself; needing you isn't the same thing as wanting to bleed you dry.
- Learn to compromise. Consider that your partner's desire to negotiate has some merit to it.
- If you are dependent, strive to do more things in your marriage without your partner's permission or help. Start small. Work to tolerate the anxiety that comes from standing on your own two feet by setting achievable goals. Learn that your independence isn't hurtful to you or to others.
- Stop blaming your partner for standing in the way of your happiness and start making plans to do whatever it will take to become happier. Make a list of the things you're the most afraid of and begin tackling them without asking for help. Make this plan as detailed as possible.

THE EFFECT OF LOSING A PARENT TO DEATH OR DIVORCE

The loss of a parent can have a profound impact on a child. Children who lose a parent to death or divorce often have problems feeling secure in their marriages. While it's easy to understand the effect of a parent's death, research shows that divorce can sometimes be even more difficult for children (Hetherington 2002). This may be because a child will feel rejected if the noncustodial parent doesn't work hard to stay close. It's also damaging to children if the custodial parent remains embittered and critical of the noncustodial parent. In addition, divorce often exposes children to other stressors such as frequent changes in living situation, decreased parental availability, and decreased financial stability (Amato 2001; Amato and Booth 1997; Crittenden 2001; Hetherington 2002; Wallerstein, Lewis, and Blakeslee 2000).

Adult children of divorce have a far greater likelihood of divorce and are less confident that their marriages will work out (Amato 2001; Amato and Booth 1997; Hetherington 2002; Wallerstein, Lewis, and Blakeslee 2000). These anxieties can cause survivors of divorce to feel more cautious, reactive, and fearful than is sometimes useful for marriage.

> Julia: My dad left when I was ten and that was almost the last I saw of him. It was really hard on me because I was a lot closer to him than I was to my mother. When he moved to Chicago, I cried myself to sleep at night for three months straight. It was really painful. I always felt like he'd show up. Plus, my mother was always talking trash about him to me; "Your dad never did give a damn about you kids. Now you know what I had to put up with all these years." That kind of crap. I lost a lot of respect for both of them.

Julia's experience with her father made it hard for her to trust men. She had a series of brief romances in her twenties and two of her marriages ended in divorce. When she came to therapy she was on the verge of her third divorce. Her third husband seemed motivated to work on the marriage; however, Julia was burning him out with her tests to see if he would reject her.

Effect on marriage of parental death or divorce

You may be burdened with fears of losing the people most important to you. Thus, you may respond by either clinging to your mate or refusing to let yourself become attached. You may feel insecure in the world and believe that something terrible is in the offing. You may test your partner by being difficult or rejecting to see if he or she is going to leave you as your parent did. You may have made a decision to go it alone in life and not depend on anyone in order never to be wounded again. This may make it impossible for your partner to be close to you. You may be overly dependent on a safe person such as a mate.

Path for change

- Evaluate whether you have grieved for the death or divorce of your parent(s). Were you comforted during the loss or did you have to manage your feelings alone? Were you able to be a child or did you have to take care of the surviving or custodial parent? Did someone help you make sense of your thoughts and feelings, or were you left bewildered and overwhelmed?
- Write a letter to the parent who died or left. Tell him or her what that was like for you and the effect it's had on you and your marriage. Let yourself feel the emotions of sadness, grief, or anger. The more in touch with your feelings you are, the less you may need to act them out in your marriage.
- Learn to become aware of your belief system by keeping a journal of your thoughts and feelings around the topic of intimacy and rejection. Develop positive counterstatements to the irrational beliefs that you hold about yourself or others.
- Take risks in your marriage and friendships. Stop waiting for your partner to change to feel safe and secure. Don't blame your partner for your difficulties with being intimate.
- Learn that you're more resilient than when you were young. Adults have a wealth of experience and healthy defenses that children lack. Even if you get rejected or lose your partner, you'll survive and grow; you're stronger than you know. Your memory of loss keeps you afraid as an adult and interferes with your taking the risks you need to change and grow.

The Need for Help and Admiration

Children need a frequent source of admiration, praise, and support in order to feel confident and calm in and outside of marriage. Parents who constantly use shame, humiliation, intimidation, or guilt trips produce children with self-esteem problems. They often become adults who are anxious or insecure in their marriages. It's much harder to do the work of marriage if you're constantly feeling one down or on the verge of being shamed or rejected.

> Pierre: My parents were very hard to please. I don't think I heard "Good job" ever. I remember being in kindergarten and showing my mother some finger painting or something that I was really proud of and she just laughed and said, "I don't think I have to worry about you running off to be an artist, because you certainly can't draw." It was pretty nonstop. "You're stupid, you're lazy, why don't you ever do anything right, why can't you be more like your brothers." A person hears that enough times, he starts to believe it.

In Pierre's marriage he was passive and resentful and his wife was critical, much like his parents. He was unable to defend himself against his wife because, unconsciously, he believed he deserved to be shamed and humiliated. Thus, he seethed inside, though he said little. His wife grew to respect him less and less over time because he didn't stand up to her and allowed himself to be mistreated by her and by others.

Experiences outside of the household can also lead to a strong feeling of defectiveness. Children who grow up with undiagnosed learning disabilities or attention deficit disorder may develop strong beliefs that they are fundamentally flawed. In addition, children who have physical features that make them the object of teasing by peers or family members can also carry strong feelings of defectiveness into their marriages. Children who grow up shorter, fatter, less attractive, who stutter, have severe acne, or are painfully shy can all internalize a strong belief that they are seriously flawed, and these insecurities can affect their behavior in marriage (Young and Klosko 1994).

Effect on marriage
You may be drawn either to a partner who would reject you, or to one you can reject. You may have a hard time feeling good about yourself, and this can make you distance yourself from your partner for fear of being hurt. You may be perfectionistic or workaholic to escape internal accusations that you're not good enough; you may also burden your spouse or children with perfectionistic expectations if you've identified with your parents' treatment. You may be excessively oriented to pleasing others at the expense of your own needs, or excessively defiant at any hint of criticism. You may be overly dependent on your partner's opinions to maintain your self-esteem because you're so hard on yourself. You may expect to be found out or revealed as a fraud. You may have a hard time relaxing or being spontaneous unless you're using substances or you're by yourself.

Path for change

- Learn to tolerate the anxiety that closeness raises. Don't run from it by rejecting or being critical of others' efforts to be close. Replace your critical beliefs about yourself with positive, self-supportive beliefs such as "I am deserving of love, attention, and admiration" and "I am a worthwhile person." Make a list of all of your strengths and achievements and use those to counter your internal criticisms.
- Identify the negative ways that you treat your partner as your parents treated you. Commit to changing this pattern. Make amends to those you have hurt.
- You may have developed an excessive need for approval as

an attempt to counter your feelings of defectiveness. Work on this by identifying your dysfunctional beliefs and countering them. Use this strategy to cultivate the awareness that you don't need others' approval to feel good about yourself. Too much seeking of approval gives your partner or others excessive control over your well-being or state of mind.

· Learn to tolerate criticism. This will require developing your self-esteem so that you don't take the criticisms to heart. In addition, learn to be assertive so that you don't feel at the mercy of toxic people, spouses or otherwise.

CONCLUSION

MANY PEOPLE FEEL disloyal to their families when asked to examine their parents' shortcomings. They often feel that their parents tried the best they could, given where they came from and what they had to work with. I think that parents, in general, *do* do the best they can. However, that's where the analysis should begin, not end. The fact that parents did the best they could or were well-intentioned doesn't always mean that they did enough, or that their good intentions were expressed in a way that was useful for the child (Coleman 2000b).

On the other hand, parents *are* sometimes blamed by therapists or politicians for things that are increasingly outside of their control. For example, studies show that poverty, race, and lower socio-economic level can give parents much less control and influence over their children (Cobb and Senett 1972). African American children are routinely discriminated against in the attitudes of their teachers, in the funding and resources of their schools, and in the quality and availability of medical care (Coontz 1992). Exposure to ongoing discrimination directly affects self-esteem, optimism, and the desire to achieve. A study at Harvard found that African American boys who scored in the *ninetieth* percentile on the Iowa achievement test in the third grade dropped down to the twenty-fourth percentile by the seventh grade.[4] This isn't poor parenting. This is large-scale institutional and societal neglect.

Conversely, upper-class and many middle-class parents are able to provide psychotherapy, tutors, boarding schools, and summer and after-school programs that can correct serious problems in parenting or vulnerabilities in the child (Ostrander 1984). They are also better able to raise their children in neighborhoods and schools where the children are safer from coercive influences. In this case, the effects of parenting can be corrected or aided by the programs of enrichment and the safety net that follows many of these children into adulthood. This doesn't mean that middle- and upper-class children are immune to parental trauma or neglect, genetic vulnerabilities, or exposure to the problematic aspects of our culture. It means that those parents are much better able to protect their children from these effects because they possess the resources that less fortunate parents lack.

However, whether from societal or parental influences, it is critical to understand how you were affected by your past and with your caregivers. Understanding these effects may increase the possibility that your marriage can be freed from their weight and influence. Changing your behavior in some of the ways described may be enough to begin to put your marriage back on track. Either way, gaining happiness in the difficult marriage comes as you begin to stop blaming your partner for your unhappiness and strive to understand how you hold yourself back in life. Inevitably, this leads us to the fertile landscape of where we need to grow and change.

4

Starting to Change

Chemistry, identity, and guilt

"Irene seemed so much like me when I first met her. Now
I feel like I don't even know who she is."
—MANNY, AGE THIRTY

"I thought Issac and I were going to be soul mates. After
eight years of marriage, I think cell mates is more like it."
—ANGELINA, AGE FORTY-ONE

PEOPLE GET MARRIED for all kinds of reasons. While love and
attraction are among the most common modern-day ingredients,
other reasons still figure high on the motivation list. These include
the desire to leave home, a need for financial security, peer or family
pressure, unplanned pregnancy, and a worry that time is running
out. Studies show that we're the most consistently attracted to people with the same religion, ethnic background, race, socioeconomic
status, age, and political views. After those qualities, the next most
consistent things in common are personality and intelligence (Diamond 1993; 1997).

Surprisingly, one of the things that we're attracted to is how similar the person looks to our parents or siblings. What? Freud was
right? Well, maybe from an evolutionary perspective. According to
physiologist Jared Diamond (1993), "On the average, spouses re-
semble each other slightly but significantly in almost every physical
feature examined." True not only of hair and eye color, weight or

skin color, but other more surprising traits as well. "Those other traits include ones as diverse as breadth of nose, length of earlobe or middle finger, circumference of wrists, distance between the eyes and lung volume! Experimenters have made this finding for people as diverse as Poles in Poland, Americans in Michigan and Africans in Chad. . . . At least unconsciously, people care more about their spouse's middle finger length than about his or her hair color and IQ! In short, like tends to marry like."

Based on these characteristics, Diamond believes that we develop our image for a future sex partner between birth and the age of six. He observes that humans are not unique in these attractions and terms this preference a *search image*. A search image is an unconscious template that guides whom and what we're attracted to.[1] However, the details of similarity between our objects of desire and our families of origin extend beyond the biological. Psychologically, we are often most attracted to people who share similar psychological characteristics with our parents and siblings. This explains the paradox that people who grow up in abusive homes are sometimes attracted to someone abusive or someone whom they can abuse. It also explains why someone who was raised by possessive or controlling parents gets involved with someone who is possessive or controlling, or responds in his or her own marriage with this behavior.

CHEMISTRY

I WAS RECENTLY REMINDED of the search image concept with a new client who wanted advice about whether to marry a man who had cheated on her twice during the past year. She said she didn't want to break up with him, because the chemistry was "unbelievable." The first time she found out about his affair, he promised not to do it again, and she forgave him. Six months later she discovered it again, this time with someone new. When I saw her, it was one month after his last incident, and he had proposed to her in the interim. He admitted that he was a sex addict but wanted to change. She wanted to know if I thought she should marry him.

I looked at this client, who was highly educated, attractive, and successful. I told her that for me to be helpful I should probably ask her a few questions about her relationship and her past. I first asked if her fiancé had gone to any meetings to help with his sex addiction. I figured that if a man was a sex addict, *and* he was going to meetings, *and* was in intensive therapy, *and* had one hell of a lot of insight into why he'd cheat on a woman twice in the course of a year when they hadn't yet even encountered the challenges of marriage and children, well, I'd be willing to consider that he *could* change. She said she didn't think he was going to meetings "or was that type." I asked if he was in therapy or if they had had couple's therapy. She said no, but maybe that was a good idea.

I asked if either of her parents had ever had affairs. "Oh yes, my father had a lot of them. It was very public. A huge mess." I didn't need to ask any more questions about her parents for the moment. I asked her why she believed her fiancé would never cheat on her again. She responded that he felt bad and didn't want to hurt her again.

"Didn't he say that the first time you found out?" I asked her.

"Yes, but he says this time it's different."

"Why do you believe him?"

"He seems sincere."

I then asked her whether, if her boyfriend were a crack addict and had had one month of sobriety, she would lend him her credit card.

"What? Of course not."

"But you'd risk getting married next month to someone who only cheated on you one month ago?"

My client was willing to ignore that her fiancé was a high-risk candidate to disappoint her in a serious way. It was not a surprise to me that her father had had affairs and that she had been hurt by them. In this case, her search image was for someone with characteristics like her father's, however troubling those characteristics were. This was a case of an alarm system remaining silent when it should have been blaring like a foghorn. She had repressed the pain and humiliation she had experienced as a result of her father's affairs, and this compromised her ability to be appropriately skeptical. She had learned in her family of origin to ignore certain signs of danger to protect her connection with her mother and father.

THE ROLE OF ANXIETY

Because our survival is tied to our parents when we're children, we're highly motivated to avoid *any* activity which will threaten our ties to them. For example, if a child observes over time that her mother becomes hurt when she behaves independently, she may, without her awareness, institute an emotional alarm system or signal that will keep her away from the danger of this loss with her mother, and later, with other relationships. Similarly, if a child is rejected whenever he is sad, he may develop an internal signal which helps him avoid feeling, expressing, or showing that emotion.

This signal is anxiety. Anxiety is a warning that something bad is about to happen (Freud 1926; Weiss and Sampson 1986; Weiss 1993). It is learned from early life experiences with parents and other important figures, such as siblings, and often stems from dysfunctional beliefs. Over time, the alarm system becomes automatic and unconscious. This can be problematic because the system was developed and encoded by a child who didn't understand a lot about the world or human behavior. Thus, your alarms are currently wired to alert you to dangers that are very likely outdated or never existed. It may scream at you to run when you're not really in danger, and be as silent as a tree stump when you should head for the hills.

My client was attracted to her fiancé because their interaction reminded her of the feelings that she had had as a child; it mimicked an earlier experience of herself that felt familiar and thus alluring. This is a version of that sometimes toxic and confusing phenomenon called "chemistry." This chemistry caused her to feel insufficient anxiety about someone who was potentially dangerous to her because it triggered the longing to be cared for by her father. And because her boyfriend had other positive qualities, she assumed that his positive qualities were the sole cause of her attraction. People like my client can get drawn into harmful and destructive relationships because they have forgotten so much of their past that they have *insufficient* anxiety. Their warning devices have been disabled or shut down.

OVERREACTIVE

The opposite can also exist, where our childhood traumas make our alarm system so sensitive that it broadcasts danger when little is there. This was true of a couple that I worked with several years ago. The husband, Maurice, had watched his mother humiliate his father with her affairs. She brought men home and told Maurice that she needed other men because his father was such a weakling. Maurice's mother left him and his father for one of these men when Maurice was twelve. His father never remarried.

Maurice was hurt by watching his father's failure to protect himself, and by his mother's abandonment. Thus, he brought into marriage a terror of being abandoned, along with a certainty of its inevitability. This caused him to police his wife's every glance, and harass her with his suspicions, despite her behaving in a trustworthy fashion. His failure to examine and work through the impact of his childhood experiences threatened to ruin his marriage. Unlike my other client's, Maurice's alarm system was so overly sensitive that it caused him to be in a constant state of red alert. The first client was about to get into a marriage that should probably have been avoided. Maurice was in danger of ruining a marriage that was worth saving.

Becoming aware of how your alarm system is set can help you gain greater control over your reactions or distortions. If you're underreactive, you may ignore or misread internal signals that you are in danger of being hurt, used, or mistreated. You don't adequately protect yourself in your marriage or relationships, and are surprised when you get betrayed, disappointed, or hurt. This may cause you to trust when you shouldn't, and try when you should give up.

If you're overreactive, you are constantly on the lookout with your spouse for slights, insults, criticisms, or rejection. This causes you either to be aggressive or to shut down and withdraw in order to decrease your partner's influence over you.

Chemistry and attraction can also be based on a desire for growth. We can be drawn to those who have, among other characteristics, the capacity to show us the way out of our restricted selves into a more full and complete self (Hendrix 1988). Thus, an unassertive man may be drawn to an assertive woman so that he can learn how to stand up for himself. A cautious woman may be drawn to an extroverted man so that she can learn to become more uninhibited. Someone who's intellectually inhibited may be attracted to someone who is confident and ambitious in his or her intellect.

DIFFERENTIATION

THE INFLUENTIAL FAMILY therapist Murray Bowen (1978) observed that we are attracted to partners who are at a similar level of psychological differentiation. Differentiation is the capacity to maintain a clear sense of self even when we're being pushed to conform or cave in to another's demands. Differentiation in marriage reflects our capacity to stay in touch with our needs, ideas, and feelings even when under pressure from a husband or wife. It's the ability to hear and accept that your partner has different requirements for happiness and meaning without feeling *unduly* obligated to address those requirements out of feelings of fear or guilt.

As an example, a well-differentiated woman might be disappointed or saddened by her husband's withdrawal of support when she decides to go back to school, but she wouldn't experience it as a threat to her identity. She wouldn't take his withdrawal to mean that she's unlovable or unworthy. A less differentiated spouse might feel panicked by this withdrawal of support and could institute more desperate behaviors to manage the painful feelings.

A study of newlyweds bears out the importance of a husband's differentiation from his family of origin. Researchers found that a husband's lack of independence from his parents resulted in poorer adjustment to the new marriage (Amstutz-Haws and Mallinckrodt 1996; Belsky and Kelly 1994). Husbands who were free from excessive feelings of guilt, mistrust, anxiety, inhibition, and anger in relation to their mothers were far more likely to adjust well to marriage. In addition, if they were able to manage practical matters without excessive help from their fathers, they were also more likely to experience greater early marital adjustment. The importance of differentiation to marital satisfaction is also why marital researcher John Gottman (1999) advises couples (especially husbands) to prioritize the needs of the marriage over the needs, requests, and requirements of their parents.

Less differentiated people sometimes have a harder time in relationships because they are more likely to feel negatively impacted by their partner's disagreement, negativity, or assertiveness in the same way that they would with their parents. A common way that some manage the anxiety of conflict or the demands of intimacy is to reduce their spouse's ability to influence them by withdrawing, physically or psychologically. They create distance by being argumentative or create conflicts as a way to avoid feeling vulnerable. They avoid the closeness of marriage through outside involvements, shutting down, communicating little, or becoming overly involved with work. They keep a partner at arm's length.

The opposite is true for those who manage the anxiety of marital conflict and intimacy by merging with a partner. This isn't the blissful merge of the early phase of a relationship; it's being psychologically unable to tolerate the ways in which your husband or wife is different. Thus, they adopt a role in marriage of dependency or constant need because those needs were so unmet in their families of origin. They may feel threatened by a partner's growth or independence because they worry that this signals a withdrawal of love, support, or interest. In marriage, they feel ruled by what is pleasing or displeasing to the spouse or, sometimes, children (Bowen 1978; Hendrix 1988).

When couples are compatible in their levels of differentiation, a satisfying relationship can ensue. For example, partners who both require a lot of reassurance and validation may be generous in their willingness to supply it to the other. Where both members prefer distance and noninvolvement, the spouses may feel comforted by the relative lack of demand that each makes for contact, conversation, or conflict resolution.

FEMALE AND MALE DIFFERENTIATION

IN THE UNITED STATES, as well as in many other Western societies, the needs of the individual are idealized, sometimes to the detriment of others. As sociologist David Popenoe writes in *Life Without Father*, "People have become strong on individual rights and weak on community obligations. In our ever-growing pursuit of the self—self-expression, self-development, self-actualization, and self-fulfillment—the social has become increasingly problematic." Even the language of psychotherapists idealizes such character traits as autonomy, independence, and individuation. In *The Anatomy of Dependence*, Japanese psychiatrist Takeo Doi observes that American culture doesn't have a way to talk about dependent behavior that isn't associated with weakness. While our society applauds rugged individualism, one's cooperative relationships with others is a greater source of self-esteem and definition in other societies. For example, in East Asian cultures, identity is largely gained from one's relationships, from one's group memberships, and from pursuing harmony with others. In some African cultures, self-esteem is gained by one's standing in the family or clan (Markus, Mullally, and Kitayama 1997). Among Hindu Indians, care for and interest in others is based on a moral code rather than a matter of personal discretion or preference (Cousins 1989; Markus and Kitayama 1991). Even within the United States, minority groups such as African Americans, Asian Americans, and Hispanics are more likely to define the individual in an interdependent way rather than as standing separate and apart from others.

In *In a Different Voice,* psychologist Carol Gilligan writes that the individualistic view of self may better define men's psychology than women's. Psychologists Susan E. Cross and Laura Madson (1997) observe that for women, "self-esteem or enhancement derive from thoughts and feelings that emphasize one's connectedness to others, from behaviors or skills that help the person fit in or harmonize with close others, and from vicarious participation in the joys and successes of self-defining others. . . . Evidence shows that women's sense of self is more contextually based and therefore more vulnerable to the disruptions [common] in distressed marriages."

Research shows that men are far more likely to describe themselves in terms of separateness from others and to derive pride from their ability to achieve that separateness. The key to men's self-esteem is frequently a perception that few of their peers do as well as they (Gorethals, Messick, and Allison 1991). By contrast, women who perform well and perceive their peers as doing likewise are more likely to feel good about themselves (Cross and Madson 1997) This is hardly to say that women are incapable of being competitive with other women (or men). For example, in *Survival of the Prettiest,* Harvard psychologist Nancy Etcoff shows that beautiful women are more likely to lose friendships with other women because others feel diminished by that beauty. In general, however, women are more likely to define themselves using the language and experience of interdependence than are men.

Thus, while the family you grow up in can affect your level of differentiation, your culture and gender also influence your experience and goals for differentiation. As a result, I commonly tell my women clients to "just pretend you're a guy" when I'm helping them strategize how to be more self-interested with their husbands or at work. In this regard, I'm helping them be less worried about hurting somebody's feelings or acting on their own behalf, since studies show that women are more vulnerable to worry and guilt (Nolen-Hoeksema and Girgus 1994). My male clients, not infrequently, need to learn how to be more tuned in to their emotions as a way of discovering how their behavior, tone, and language affect those around them in marriage or at work. Both genders have a lot to learn from the other.

These differences between the sexes directly translate into how comfortable each is in navigating the ever-shifting resource pool of marriage. Many women's financial dependence on their husbands makes them feel less entitled to do the kind of hard-nosed horse trading that is sometimes required to negotiate for one's happiness in marriage (Crittenden 2001). Women's ability to be more tuned in to what a partner is thinking and feeling (Robertson, Rooke, and Teng 1986) may also make them more vulnerable to feeling burdened. If women are more vulnerable to guilt and worry, then they may be more likely to inhibit making decisions that are in their best interest, out of a desire to avoid making a partner unhappy. Men's ability to compartmentalize makes them more insulated from marital demands and therefore less at risk when they want to assert their needs. However, this ability to feel comfortably separate also makes them less aware of their own needs for connection. It makes them more likely to be caught off guard by their wives' feelings of resentment, hurt, or disappointment and may explain why marital researcher Mavis Hetherington (2002) found that a full one-fourth of her sample of divorced men were completely surprised when their wives announced their intention to seek a divorce.

Ultimately, finding or maintaining happiness while married is a process of differentiation because it requires you to stay in touch with who you are in the face of feeling hurt, neglected, frustrated, or even betrayed by your partner. The painful beauty of marriage is that it provides plenty of opportunities for this kind of personal growth. This is why it's so important to understand how your childhood affected you. Your ability to define yourself independently of your partner's feedback is tied to how clearly your parents saw you. For example, a woman who was consistently told that she was selfish growing up found herself unable to act in a self-interested way with her husband because of this belief, especially when he accused her of being selfish. It was only as she was able to understand the effect of her parents' feedback that she was able to behave with her partner in a way that maintained her happiness. Similarly, a man who was called weak by his parents for wanting affection or reassurance as a child was unable to pursue intimacy with his wife out of a fear of being accused of these qualities. As he began to see the irrationality of these beliefs he was better able to initiate intimacy with his wife. If he had been married to a woman who was incapable of intimacy, he would have needed to be sufficiently differentiated from his wife to develop and maintain his self-esteem in the absence of her feedback.

GUILT: THE OBSTACLE TO CHANGE

PEOPLE CONSTANTLY STRIVE to master the beliefs and experiences that cause them to feel inhibited in their lives and marriages (Weiss and Sampson 1986; Zeitlin 1991; Vogel 1994). Thus, someone who enters marriage in a dependent state may continually work toward increased independence. Similarly, someone who enters marriage with an anxious need for independence in relationships may gradually work toward more interdependence in his marriage.

Often, conflicts begin to surface when people start to change the dynamic of the relationship. As one member of a couple begins to change or grow, the other may begin to raise the stakes to keep the marriage mired in the old patterns. If a partner's dependency or passivity wasn't a problem in the marriage before, her becoming stronger may be. When a wife that I worked with decided to go back to school, her husband felt threatened by it and told her they couldn't afford it. When she said she'd borrow the money from her parents, he accused her of trying to humiliate him by making him look bad in her parents' eyes. She offered to borrow it through a bank and he told her she wasn't responsible with money and he'd be left holding the bag. When she made it clear that she would find a way to do it, he told her she was being a bad mother to leave the kids at home while she pursued her own interests.

My client eventually learned to calmly assert herself with her husband, but it took a long time. When he expressed discouragement at her going back to school she felt overwhelmed with feelings of guilt. Even though she could rationally perceive that going back to school was not a selfish act, her spouse made her choose between her own aspirations and his desires. This made her feel anxious that she would lose his love. She needed to take the risk that she could survive, regardless of the effect of her actions on him. In other words, she needed to become better differentiated from her husband. To do this, she had to gain control of the following irrational beliefs:

- I should always put others' needs before mine.
- I don't deserve to develop my own interests and ambitions.
- My own needs are selfish and petty.
- A woman's role in life is to make her man feel good about himself, even if it hurts her to do so.
- If I try to make myself happy I'll get hurt, and I can't tolerate that.

TOWARD INTERDEPENDENCE

SOMETIMES GROWTH ISN'T toward increased independence, but toward an increased capacity to be intimate and interdependent. If distance and lack of emotion aren't a problem in a marriage, it may mean that *both* partners have an unconscious agreement to maintain a certain level of distance. When one person changes, it upsets this balance, and problems can ensue.

> Mark: I was pretty disconnected from my feelings when I met Lori. A lot of women complained that I never talked, but I think Lori kinda liked that about me. Anyway, after my dad died I got a lot more in touch with everything I'd been stuffing all of my life and really wanted to talk to her about it and everything else. I started seeing how much I was like him as a dad, kind of distant and critical. Lori freaked. I think it scared her to see me act like I needed her instead of being this super-independent guy that I was before. It pissed me off, actually. I felt like, "Oh, you get to be all emotional, but if I have an emotion then that's another story."

It was another story. Lori had grown up in a chaotic home with two out-of-control parents. Both mother and father were alcoholic and violent. Lori liked Mark's quietness because it suggested someone who would never get out of control in the frightening way that her parents did. When Mark began to change and wanted to express more of his emotions, Lori became scared that he would turn into her parents. This caused her to withdraw from him and act rejecting when he wanted to talk about his emotions. She did this by accusing him of being weak and needy. Mark responded to this criticism by withdrawing further from Lori and retreating back to his unemotional state before his father's death.

THE GATEKEEPER

SELF-CHANGE CAN RAISE issues similar to those in adolescence. Thus, as you begin to change in your marriage, you may believe that you have to storm and break down the walls of your partner's resistance in order to win your freedom. This often means that you'll attempt to manage the guilt and anxiety that your partner's reactions elicit in you by blaming or withdrawing. You may become critical of your partner as a first step to gaining independence, much in the way our teenagers do of us. You may be tempted to view your *partner* as the obstacle to growth instead of seeing your own reactions to his behavior as the obstacle.

This is a key point in gaining happiness in any marriage. Many people suffer because they give up pursuing activities or experiences in response to their spouse's objections. They waste precious years saying to themselves, "If only my spouse were different, I could do or feel *x*." Others don't pursue what would make them happy because they *think* their partner wouldn't like it, even though their spouse hasn't even had the chance to object because the requests were never put on the table.

It's also important to recognize that your spouse *may* lose something in the bargain when you grow or change. We often deny this because we fear that if we empathize with our partner's feelings, we'll lose touch with our own. Making a husband or wife bad, wrong, or inadequate reduces the pull we feel from them. It's a way of saying, "Why should I care about what you say? You're too big of a jerk for me to care." Anger can provide the sometimes useful fuel of self-righteousness to reduce the downward pull of guilt. "I *never* do or get what I want. You *always* get to do what you want. I'm tired of doing everything for everybody else and *nothing* for myself! I'm going to focus on *me* this time." I often observe that as someone begins to become assertive, she swings all of the way into aggressiveness first. This aggressiveness can help her feel safer as she treads into new waters. It's like walking into a dangerous situation with a weapon pointed out in front of you; it's not until you know that you're safe that you feel comfortable checking your gun at the door.

While it's possible that your growth is threatening to your spouse, it's also possible that you believe this to be true and you're wrong, especially if you believe that your partner is acting just like your parents. Either way, if you feel guilty about how your behavior affects your partner, you will experience yourself as having to aggressively wrest yourself away from his clutches by counterblaming, shaming, or rejecting. This can be problematic in most homes because it produces a cycle where your partner responds to your counterblame by blaming back, thereby confirming your worst fears. In general, as you feel more comfortably entitled to change, you will feel less need to angrily justify your decisions. Remaining calmly committed to change without blaming back short-circuits this cycle and increases your feeling of differentiation from your partner.

TESTING IN MARRIAGE

ONE OF THE KEY ways that people begin to differentiate in marriage is through testing. As couples begin to be more comfortable with each other, they begin to unconsciously test their partners in increasingly challenging ways. This is also a way that we continue to differentiate from our parents, by seeing if their opinions of us are shared by other important people. According to psychoanalyst Joseph Weiss, testing serves to master the irrational, symptom-producing beliefs that are developed primarily in childhood in response to incorrect inferences from relationships with parents or other important family members (Weiss and Sampson 1986).

For example, a woman with rejecting parents might test in her marriage by being extremely difficult. This would serve to master the irrational belief that she deserves to be rejected.

Jody's mother had three divorces over the course of today's childhood. She had very little contact with her father or with her stepfathers after the divorces. When she became married, she was terrified that she'd be abandoned in the same way that her father and stepfathers abandoned her. As a result, she was extremely difficult with her husband until she became reassured that she couldn't drive him away.

Jody's difficult behavior was a way to test her husband to see if she could drive him away. Unconsciously, she believed that it was her fault that her father and stepfathers left her. As she became more confident that her behavior wasn't going to cause her husband to leave, she was able to stop testing him in this way. However, this isn't the way it always goes. If Jody's husband had been equally fearful of rejection, he might have been scared away by her difficult behavior and responded by rejecting her back, thereby confirming her worst fears about herself. In that scenario, they would likely have become mired in conflict and misunderstanding.

Testing is also illustrated by the case of Patrick and Denise. Patrick was a quiet and shy research scientist who was married to Denise, a litigation attorney. When Patrick was growing up, his parents demanded absolute allegiance to them. Disagreement was tantamount to betrayal. He recalled an incident when his mother cried after he mildly differed with her at dinner over the Gulf War when her friends were over. She tearfully told him that he had humiliated her in public and made her feel terrible about herself. As a result of many interactions like this with his parents, he developed a set of dysfunctional beliefs that could be summed up as "Disagreeing with others is hurtful and selfish." Over time, he became oriented to pleasing and complying with others' needs, and stifling his own feelings of criticism or independence.

Patrick loved Denise's assertiveness because she showed that it can be an expression of strength and pleasure, not selfish hurtfulness. Unconsciously, it gave him a way to repair and replace what was missing in himself. However, as is common in marriage, Patrick eventually became upset with the very thing he was attracted to in his wife. Over time he began to feel trapped by Denise's assertiveness when she began to tell him how she wanted him to be with her, sexually. He described her behavior in the following way; "She's kind of castrating. She'll say, I really need a lot more foreplay to get stimulated. Touch me like this!' I just don't like her telling me how I'm supposed to make love to her. It's like, let me do it how I want to do it. Let me be in charge of this."

Patrick was wrongly perceiving that Denise was like his parents, demanding and possessive, instead of comfortably self-interested. As a result, he began to behave with Denise in the same way that his parents had behaved with him. Thus, he projected a negative intention onto her healthy behavior of directly asking for what she wanted, in this case, in bed. This kept him loyal and aligned with his parents. It was as if he were saying to Denise, "We Smiths don't go for that sort of self-interested behavior." In being loyal to his parents, he kept repressed the memory of how painful it was when they took this stance with him. In other words, if this was just "how it's done in the world," then he had nothing to feel sad or angry about from his childhood. If he was deprived by his parents, well, that's a different story.

Some common areas that people test in marriage involve a fear of being used, unappreciated, controlled, betrayed, rejected, devalued, shamed, or humiliated. It's important to understand how you may be testing in your marriage, for these strategies may keep you mired in conflict and unhappiness if you misinterpret your partner's reactions, or if you fail to understand what you are attempting to master through your behavior.

SOME QUESTIONS TO CONSIDER

YOU MAY HAVE outgrown your partner in some important way and thus need to work on accepting the limitations of your marriage. However, there may be a lot more you should do before making that decision. The following questions will help you evaluate this:

- How guilty do you feel about changes you have made or want to make in your life?
- How do you manage the guilt that this raises?
- How much time have you spent reassuring your partner that the changes you want to make are not because you find your partner boring, repulsive, dependent, or annoying? Even if you find your partner to be all of those things, you would have to communicate your feelings in a way that takes responsibility for your reactions rather than blaming him or her. We're all exquisitely sensitive to shifts in our spouse's behavior, and any change has the potential to stimulate anxiety in the other. This anxiety could cause your partner to behave in a way that confirms your worst fears. While your partner shouldn't have veto power over your growth, you are more likely to get participation or less resistance from your spouse if you can be sensitive and empathic to his or her reactions to it.
- In what ways are you threatened by your partner's growth? There may be aspects of your partner's health that you are drawn to but seek to limit or sabotage because it makes you feel more insecure, anxious, or afraid. It may also be that the negative feelings you have toward your partner are the places where you need to learn the most about yourself. As psychiatrist Peter Kramer (1997) writes, "It is the complexity, the impossibility, the dullness, or painfulness of the current imperfect relationship that provides the context for change." And in the words of Søren Kierkegaard (1998 [1847]), "Perfect love means to love the one through whom one became unhappy."

CONCLUSION

REGARDLESS OF THE influences, finding happiness in the difficult marriage is a process of differentiation. This means reducing your partner's ability to influence your identity and self-esteem in the areas where it's painful to you. Marriage is an arena where you are forced to continue the work on becoming the self that you began with your parents. If you were loved unconditionally as a child, you may feel freer in marriage to resist the accusations and feelings of guilt or anxiety that come as you begin to grow and change. If you are burdened with beliefs that you are selfish, unlovable, unworthy, or unimportant, you will have to work harder to resist those messages as you begin to change yourself and the dynamic in your marriage.

In other words, you enter marriage able to be as fully yourself as you have learned it is safe to be. The person you reveal to a spouse is often an incomplete version, a half-truth of who you really are, a self that remains hidden to your partner, let alone to you. When the inevitable push comes to shove of needing to change in order to be happy, you come face-to-face with those areas where you feel the most scared, angry, and inhibited. If your marriage makes you depressed or you struggle with depression, this change can feel much more difficult to enact.

5

Depression in Marriage

Is it me, my partner, or the marriage?

"My marriage is the main thing that I get depressed about. Other than that, I'm fine."
—MARA, AGE TWENTY-SEVEN

"I have a really hard time living with my wife's depression. Some days I just want to say, 'Can you just be happy about something for one day?' I really get tired of it. She really brings me down."
—RONNIE, AGE THIRTY-SEVEN

"I've been depressed most of my life. When I met Marvin, I was happy for the first time. But, the problems in our marriage make me feel as depressed as ever. I don't know whether it's him or me, but something's gotta change."
—SHARLENA, AGE FORTY-NINE

KATHERINE WAS A HIGH-SCHOOL TEACHER in her mid-thirties. On the phone, scheduling her first appointment, she said that she was thinking about leaving her husband, had pretty much made up her mind about it, but wanted to make sure it was the right thing. When she entered my office she sat down and confidently went into her story. I had the experience of sitting before someone with whom I already had a long friendship. She was funny, charming, and engaging. She said that she had outgrown her husband and if it weren't for the kids she would have left long ago.

I asked about her husband. "He's an engineer. He's a good guy.

I know it's really terrible to say, but he's boring. When I met him, I was a lot more needy and he helped me grow because he's really accepting and I needed that. I mean, I feel like a creep for wanting to leave, but I need a lot more than he can give."

"What do you feel like you're not getting?"

"Passion, excitement. I know that changes with marriage over time, but c'mon, it's gotta be more than this."

As she spoke, I sorted through my hypotheses. I considered that the truth was just as she was constructing it: Woman marries man who's a parental figure, outgrows him, and later feels lonely because she wants more of an equal. While this wouldn't necessarily mean that she *should* leave her husband, it might mean that she *would* have to decrease her expectations of what her marriage was going to be like.

In addition, I was struck by the unusual ease with which she was presenting herself. Despite the appeal, I wondered if she had to hide other parts of herself in order to be so engaging. I asked about her childhood history and learned that she had had a lifelong struggle with depression. She had grown up the eldest of nine children and had a parental-like responsibility for the care of her siblings. Her parents were poor; her father, clinically depressed. She had never tried antidepressants, though she'd thought a lot about doing so. I considered that she might not appear depressed because she was adept at presenting herself in a reassuringly positive way, as is common for people who grow up with a lot of responsibility, finely attuned to others' needs.

DEPRESSION IN MARRIAGE

PART OF BEING HUMAN is the day-to-day navigation of slights, injuries, and disappointments: the humiliation of being passed over for a promotion or career advance, the cut of a friend's insensitive remarks, the rebuke over behavior that was intended as playful, the embarrassment of having our attentions ignored. This complex world of relationships is a more troubling and treacherous enterprise if you're weighed down with depression, ongoing anxiety, or burdensome feelings of oversensitivity.

Nowhere is this more true than in marriage, where so much of our feedback centers around one person. Depression can make you unable to enjoy marriage, parenting, work, or friendships. You can enter a marriage suffering from lifelong depression and later decide that it's your spouse that caused you to feel that way. Or you might enter marriage in a happy state and discover your or your partner's vulnerability to depression much later. Then again, maybe it's just the problems in your marriage that make you depressed.

Regardless of the source, it's tempting to blame a partner for our unhappiness. Any of us, no matter what condition our marriage, can list behaviors that our spouses could add or get rid of that might make us happier: make more money, be more sexual, lighten up, take more responsibility. The problem with depression is that you're more likely to overvalue the gain that you would enjoy from those changes. This is one of the reasons remarriages are often unsuccessful and affairs rarely turn into satisfying long-term relationships.

Research shows that one-half of women who are unhappy with their primary relationships are depressed (Kiccolt-Glaser and Newton 2001). This may be because women are more likely to define themselves in the context of a relationship and so may be more likely to gain or lose self-esteem on the basis of how well a relationship is going (Jordan and Surrey 1986). Both men and women in difficult relationships are twenty-five times more likely to be depressed than those who aren't. And this doesn't count mania or low-level depressions (Kramer 1997). Thus, both sexes are vulnerable to becoming depressed when a marriage is difficult.

According to the *Diagnostic and Statistical Manual of Mental Disorders* (2000), if you or your partner are depressed, then you may suffer from some or all of the following:

Ongoing problems with anxiety

Extreme sensitivity to criticism and rejection

Social avoidance or withdrawal

Emotional outbursts of sadness, fear, anger, or self-loathing

Extreme feelings of guilt

Severe self-doubt, perfectionism, or need for control

Problems with sleep, energy, or appetite

Low self-esteem

Decreased sexual desire and pursuit of pleasure

I asked Katherine more about her history with depression to determine whether she was currently depressed. She admitted that she had problems with sleep and felt sad more of the time than she wanted, but she assumed this was because she felt lonely in her marriage. I asked if she always felt so pessimistic about Daniel, her husband. She admitted that the feeling came and went, but she believed that when she didn't feel pessimistic, it was because she was covering over her dissatisfaction in the same way that her mother had with her father. She said that she had mistaken her husband's cautious quality for stability when she was needier, but now she saw him more clearly.

I admitted that that was a possibility, and that we would carefully investigate it together. Over the next few months I began to consider that maybe that wasn't the whole story. I told her that since her father had had a major depression, she could be more vulnerable to it, biochemically, from having him as a role model, and from being raised by a depressed parent. In addition, even without her father's depression, her role in a large, poor family with parents who were overwhelmed and unavailable could lead to adult depression.

I also considered this diagnosis for Katherine because her portrayal of her husband began to seem more sympathetic as the months passed with my working with her. He had been very supportive of her growth over the years, and continued to emotionally support her as she became more demanding and assertive. I got the image of the husband as someone who was careful, though not without strength and depth. It's true that she might prefer someone more outgoing or exciting. But it could also mean that the strength of her dissatisfaction with him was being fueled by the downward pull of her depression.

As the diagnosis seemed clearer, I suggested that she might benefit from a trial of antidepressants and referred her to a psychiatrist for a medication evaluation. The psychiatrist concurred and put her on Zoloft. Over the next month, she began to report feeling less sad and disgruntled. As she became less depressed, she began to feel more interested in her life. She also described feeling more in touch with the strengths in her husband and less preoccupied with his problems. She still talked about the fantasy of being with someone who was more adventurous and risk-taking; however, she stopped being preoccupied with Daniel's inadequacies. She became more focused on the ways that she was avoiding risk or adventure in her *own* life. She began to feel more accepting and less troubled by the same behaviors that had seemed worthy of divorce several months before.

In *Should You Leave?* psychiatrist Peter Kramer discusses the role that depression can have in causing people to negatively evaluate a marriage. "A patient may tell me that he and his wife communicate poorly, find sex together pedestrian, disagree over career, or parenting goals, or religious precepts, no longer share common interests, and squabble incessantly over issues of power and control. I will take those claims of incompatibility to be as nothing if I believe that he or his wife is, at base, depressed."

WOMEN AND DEPRESSION

ONE OUT OF EVERY seven women suffers from depression at some point in her lifetime (Kiecolt-Glaser and Newton 2001). Numerous studies have shown that marriage may be a factor, since marital stress appears to be harder on women than on men (Kiecolt-Glaser and Newton 2001). According to the University of California *Berkeley Wellness Newsletter* 18, no 1 (October 2001), a Duke University study found that married working women, aged twenty-five to forty-five experienced increases in blood pressure when there were problems at home, while their husbands did not; and a Stockholm study found that women with high marital stress were three times more likely to have a second heart attack than those in happy marriages.

There are several theories about why women are more vulnerable to depression and the stresses of a difficult marriage. Women are more encouraged to internalize angry or aggressive feelings with self-blame, isolation, or somaticization, whereas externalizing in men is more acceptable. This socialization appears to occur quite young. Boys are typically rewarded by their peers for aggressive behavior, whereas girls are more likely to experience rejection by their social group for this behavior, and then censure themselves as a result (Cross and Madson 1997). Researchers who believe that social explanations more greatly account for gender differences in depression also point to Amish and Jewish societies, where women have greater equality, and perhaps because of this, suffer from lower rates of depression and alcoholism (Leibenluft 1998).

Men appear to be less troubled by marital distress than women. This may be because, among other things, men are socialized more toward autonomy and separateness. However, this shouldn't be construed to mean that men need their wives any less. In fact, men appear to do worse with bachelorhood, divorce, and widowhood than most women. Nonmarried women have a 50 percent greater likelihood of mortality, while men in this category have a 250 percent increased chance of mortality (Kiecolt-Glaser and Newton 2001). One reason may be that men rely on their wives to schedule doctor appointments, cajole them into self-care, monitor diets, etc. In addition, wives are often the major, or sole, source of social support for many men, while women typically have a much broader network of support (Phillipson 1997). Thus, women appear to be more vulnerable when they are in a relationship, and men when they are not.

Women's conflicts between time with their children and time with their careers are also a major source of stress. Hochschild (1989) observes that while women experience an increase in self-esteem as a result of working, they are also much more burdened by not having a concomitant decrease in responsibilities at home. Many women find that when their work responsibilities end, the exhausting second shift of child and household duties when they get home begins. The combination of these pressures may also make women more vulnerable to depression.

WOMEN, CHILD ABUSE, AND DEPRESSION

ACCORDING TO THE NATIONAL ALLIANCE for the Mentally Ill, women are twice as likely as men to experience sexual abuse in childhood, and this almost always leads to depression as an adult. Recent studies show that child abuse, sexual or otherwise, causes changes in the developing brain that follow children into adulthood. Research by Martin Teicher (2002) and his colleagues at Harvard Medical School and McLean Hospital in Belmont, Massachussets, showed that child abuse can affect the development of the limbic system in the brain, the area that plays an important role in the regulation of memory and emotion. Teicher and numerous other researchers found that early child abuse can reduce the size of the hippocampus, that part of the brain involved in retrieving verbal and emotional memories. This area may be vulnerable to changes because it has a higher concentration of receptors for the stress hormone, cortisol, than other areas of the brain. Another reason why women may be more vulnerable to depression than men is because estrogen increases production of cortisol and may decrease cortisol's ability to shut itself down.[1]

Another biological explanation for the different rates of depression in women and men may relate to production of the neurotransmitter serotonin. Researchers at McGill University discovered that women produce only about one-half the amount of serotonin as men (Leibenluft 1998). (Neurotransmitters are the chemicals in the brain that allow your cells to exchange information with one another.) Low serotonin production is associated with increased risk of depression or anxiety. Popular antidepressants such as Prozac, Effexor, and Paxil, to name a few, all work by increasing the amount of serotonin in the brain. This research is new and developing. However, sex differences in the production of serotonin may explain why men respond to stress with aggression and externalizing behaviors while women respond to it with depression or anxiety.

MEN AND DEPRESSION

MEN ARE MORE LIKELY to respond to stress or depression with anger, criticism, blame, or violence (Leibenluft 1998; Real 1997). For this reason, male depression is often hard for professionals and family members to recognize. As psycholinguist Deborah Tannen writes in *You Just Don't Understand*, "If women speak and hear a language of connection and intimacy, men speak and hear a language of status and independence."[2]

I often see this in my first hour with couples who are beginning therapy together. Women commonly want to get to the details of the relationship, while men often want to talk first about their achievements or strengths. They may also want to tell me how much they don't believe in therapy or express doubt that therapy (or I, the therapist) will do them any good. As a man, I recognize these initial salvos as the male form of "Hello" and welcome them as an opportunity to connect with a husband. I know that most men need to reveal their strengths and see that they're not in danger of being humiliated before they will want to talk about their areas of vulnerability. Hurrying a man into talking about his problems before he's had the chance to talk about his abilities is almost always counterproductive.

However, outside of a therapy office, men's difficulty with disclosing vulnerability is a huge problem and a big contributor to their unhappiness. As Terrence Real writes in his 1997 book on male depression, *I Don't Want to Talk About It,* "The cultivation of a stance of invulnerability robs men of a wisdom known to most women in this culture, that people connect better when they expose their weakness." Cultural and evolutionary forces make it harder for men to show or discuss weakness, vulnerability, or need.

Tannen (1990) notes that men in the home, including nondepressed men, are more likely to be silent or nonverbally interactive, whereas women seek and prefer conversation. This difference also complicates the diagnosis and treatment of male depression. If men don't talk much under the best of circumstances, they will disclose even less during periods of depression. While many if not most wives would welcome their husbands' talking about their feelings of depression, *any* feelings, many men have found the outside world to be less tolerant of their vulnerability. An example was provided in a study by Hammen and Peters (1978), who found that when male students disclosed depression to their college roommates, they were met with social isolation and outright hostility, while women were met with caring and nurturing.

Male depression may hide behind other syndromes, such as drug and alcohol abuse, gambling, sex addiction, or violence, where men are more greatly represented than women. Male depression seems more equal to women's when we consider that men are four times more likely to kill themselves, and hospitalized male psychiatric patients greatly outnumber female patients in their rate of violent incidents. If you factor the incidences of addiction and violence into the equation, men and women may get depressed in equal numbers (Real 1997).

Paul: I basically hate the world when I'm depressed. I used to never even think of it as depression till I got arrested for battery and had to go to an anger-management class as a result. This dude there said that men handle depression through anger, which I guess is me; made me think of my old man, who was pissed off all of the time, blaming everybody else for why his life was so messed up. I can definitely get like that. My wife walked out on me twice because she was so afraid of me. The last time she said, "You get into therapy and deal with this thing or me and the kids are gone." I knew that she meant it this time, so I started dealing with it.

Family members may not recognize when a husband or father is depressed. They may assume that his irritability, moodiness, aggression, or addiction stems from personality traits rather than maladaptive attempts to manage painful feelings.

Marie: I would never have known that Neal was depressed till he wound up in the hospital over his alcoholism. I always just thought he was a prick who yelled to get his way. I grew up around men like that so I can't say it seemed unusual to me. My brothers were always fighting and my dad wasn't any better than they were. So I just figured, that's a man for you. But since he's been in recovery I can see that he's depressed underneath all that bluster. I would never have known it before.

Sometimes family members have a difficult time talking to a man about depression because of a concern that he will feel shamed or humiliated by it.

Sharla: I've known for a long time Dick was depressed, but you can't tell him that. Whenever I'd suggest counseling or anything like that he'd always say, "I don't need someone else telling me how to live my life. That's for weak people like you."

He'd never say he was depressed. He'd mostly just say that he was pissed off about this or that or "sick and tired of so and so." If I told him I thought he was depressed he'd get furious at me, like I was calling him a weakling.

LIVING WITH A DEPRESSED SPOUSE

RESEARCH SHOWS THAT living with a depressed partner is hard on the nondepressed partner. Marriages where one member is depressed are nine times more likely to end in divorce (Rosen and Amador 1996). This may be because depression causes people to divorce from partners who are more suitable than the depression allows them to see. It may also be because when one partner is depressed, the nondepressed partner is more at risk to become depressed, anxious, or phobic (Benazon and Coyne 2000). They are also more prone to experience ongoing feelings of frustration, anger, or hopelessness (Rosen and Amador 1996).

On the other hand, a depressed partner may lack the energy or drive to leave a marriage that he might otherwise leave. In addition, a nondepressed spouse might stay in a marriage he would otherwise leave out of feelings of worry about how divorce would impact the other.

Being around a depressed person may be difficult for people other than the spouse. Research shows that strangers who spent time with a depressed stranger were more likely to report feelings of anxiety and hostility than when they spent time around a nondepressed stranger. In addition, they expressed an unwillingness to spend time with the depressed person in the future (Rosen and Amador 1996).

We are wired to be responsive to those we live with. In the same way we're unable to ignore an infant's cry, we are programmed to be attuned to the ups and downs of those around us. It's evolution's way to make sure that we work for the survival of those closest to us. However, the key to becoming happy in a difficult marriage is developing a capacity to reverse that pull. Imperfect harmony sometimes involves learning how to become more immune to the mood and behavior of your partner when you need to—that is, to be sufficiently differentiated so that you aren't unduly influenced by his or her ups and downs. It's feeling entitled to be in a good mood when your partner isn't, to pursue goals that create meaning in your life, even if your spouse doesn't share that particular meaning or prefers you wouldn't pursue that particular goal.

Jeremy was a fifty-year-old musician. He had been married for twenty-five years to Sarah. They had three teenage children. Sarah was diagnosed with postpartum depression after their first child but refused to go on antidepressants. While her depression lessened a little over time, Jeremy stated that she had never returned to herself before their first child. Her sister told him in confidence that Sarah had been depressed and somewhat difficult all of her life.

Jeremy had adopted a caretaking role in his marriage. Sarah's depression caused her to be sensitive to criticism in a way that he found burdensome and suffocating. "The other night Sarah wanted me to call her best friend and yell at her because she had said something that hurt her feelings when they had lunch. Okay, it's pretty easy to hurt Sarah's feelings, and I think she totally mistook what her friend said. They've been friends forever and she's going to ruin this friendship over some comment that she might have not meant? So I'm like, 'Honey, no. You and Ruth have been friends for years; what possible good is it going to do if I call her up and yell at her for some comment,' at which point she immediately starts screaming at the top of her lungs about how I'm not loyal and I care about everybody else's feelings except hers and how her boyfriend in college would do what she wanted and that was the only thing that would make her feel better. Jesus. She just flips out sometimes. I end up feeling like I'm being a prick if I don't do the exact thing that she wants me to do, and it's really burning me out."

COPING WITH A PARTNER'S INAPPROPRIATE DEMANDS

It shouldn't take a heroic effort on your part to maintain your partner's sense of well-being or stability. This is true whether your partner is depressed or challenging in some of the other ways I discuss throughout the book. If your partner makes you feel as if you have to turn yourself into a pretzel in order for him or her to feel stable, something's wrong. If you buy into it, it may mean that something in your past makes you believe that part of the bargain of relationships is that you have to give more than you receive. Or you chose someone who is a little or a lot troubled as a way to make sure that you weren't the one who was going to be rejected. Understanding your own motivation will help you disentangle yourself from whatever accusations or demands are leveled against you as you negotiate a healthier dynamic with your spouse.

It's a good rule of thumb to remain empathic even when you're refusing to do what your partner is requesting. I know this is a tall order and you'll blow it sometimes. But the more you can be in control of your emotions, the more your spouse will be able to see himself more objectively. If you escalate into a fight, then the issue becomes about whatever critical thing you said. If you remain calm and affectionately detached, then your partner will be better able to see his behavior as separate from you.

Many people feel insincere or phony using empathic techniques when they're feeling critical or angry. They have the belief that the very temporary relief that comes from expressing genuine feelings of anger, criticism, or resentment has something to do with moving a marriage forward. This is likely because of the sixties emphasis on "getting it all out" and the current culture of "being real." However, the opposite is typically true. There is a place for expressing anger and resentment. However, it's not when you're in the midst of trying to contain the behavior of a difficult spouse. It is critical for you to be less reactive and more thoughtful about the effect of your responses, especially with a depressed partner, and especially when your marriage is challenging.

Partners who are overly demanding because of depression or some other malady often know that they are out of control. While it may temporarily scare or infuriate your partner to see you maintain your ground, it gives her an important opportunity to examine her reactions in a way that your counterreacting doesn't. To reiterate, gaining happiness in marriage has to do with developing the ability to separate your thoughts and feelings from your partner's. If your partner is depressed, your task is to maintain clarity about who you are while your spouse goes through considerable changes in mood.

As you work on yourself, you might find it useful to consider how your view of yourself has changed as a result of your partner's depression and problematic behavior. Which of the following is true for you?

I've become more withdrawn.
I've become more depressed.
I feel guilty all of the time.
I feel selfish when I do things I want to do without him.
I don't do things that I want to do because I don't want her
    to feel left out or jealous.
I've taken on more household or financial responsibility than
    feels fair to me.
I've given up on sex.
I feel like a therapist rather than a partner.
I feel as if it's my fault and if she were married to someone
    else she'd be a lot happier.
I worry a lot about him.
I feel lonely in the marriage.

It's important to recognize the ways that you have changed as a result of your partner's depression. It may mean that you have given up important parts of yourself that need to be reclaimed in order to be happy. Why would your partner's depression have such a burdensome effect on you? Depression is a withdrawal into the self. It causes a deficit in the ongoing desire for feedback and interaction. Even when depression is acted out with anger, addiction, or sensation seeking, as is common with men, it's rarely in the service of the relationship. These behaviors leave the nondepressed partner feeling lonely, helpless, guilt-ridden, and angry.

Mirroring is the process in which we get a reflection of who we are based on the reactions we receive from others. It's through the process of mirroring that a self develops out of infancy (Winnicott 1958). Empathy is a part of mirroring where we show someone that we know what he or she is feeling by reflecting those same feelings in our expression, tone, or language. Studies show that having a depressed mother can be problematic for infants and young children (Murray, Cooper, and Stein 1991; Murray 1992; Seligman et al. 1984). This is probably because depressed mothers are not only too withdrawn or burdened to care for their children, they can't mirror a lot either. Donald Nathanson (1992) has shown that if an infant smiles at a mother and the mother turns away, the infant behaves in a way that is similar to adult shame; that is, it reddens and withdraws.

While adults don't require the same level of reflection, *mirroring is an important part of the day-to-day feedback that we desire from those closest to us.* The absence of good mirroring in a marriage can increase feelings of loneliness, alienation, and despair. It can make you feel as if your partner doesn't care about your dreams or trials.

Marlene: The other day I came home from work and I was so excited because I had just found out that I had won a national prize for my artwork! I came into the living room where he was lying down and I said, "Ron! I won it! I took first place with my sculpture!" He said, "You did? That's great," but he said it with as much enthusiasm as if I had told him I just emptied the Kitty Litter. I immediately felt like, "Well, screw you too. I've only worked for something like this all of my life." Rather than feeling happy, I ended up feeling depressed, sort of like I was bragging or making too big of a deal out of it. I know his depression isn't personal, but sometimes knowing that doesn't really help. You just kind of want the person who's supposed to care to actually show you some feeling.

LONELINESS

Because depression is a retreat into the self, the nondepressed partner can feel left out and isolated. He or she may feel a deep sense of loneliness because the depressed partner is unavailable for the kinds of interactions that characterize a satisfying marriage.

Briana: Shawn gets depressed a lot and I often feel like a single parent. He sleeps a lot on the weekends, and when he comes home from work he spends most of the evening before bed watching television. I know he's depressed and I've racked my brain to try to make him happy. I feel like if I was a good wife I'd be able to figure something out, but I haven't. I say, "Let's go see a movie, let's go out to dinner, let's go away for the weekend," but it's always, "No, I don't feel like it. Do what you want." He won't talk about his depression even though it's obvious that he has it. It makes me jealous of my friends who are always going away with their husbands or doing things. I get tired of feeling alone in my marriage.

Excessive worry about a depressed spouse can weigh down a marriage. Worry can tempt you to inhibit goals or activities in an attempt not to stress or burden your depressed partner. It can also leave you feeling inadequate and guilty over not being able to help.

HELPLESSNESS

Living with a depressed spouse can make you depressed, angry, and discouraged because of your inability to help. Psychologist Martin Seligman (1991) has shown that depression results from the experience of helplessness while repeatedly pursuing a goal. Thus, you are likely to blame yourself, feel inadequate, or accuse yourself of being a bad spouse if your partner is depressed. A depressed person can also become hostile, critical, shaming, and humiliating. This can leave the nondepressed partner feeling worthless and vulnerable.

NEEDINESS

People whom others label as "needy" are frequently depressed. That's because the depressed person *does* need more—more reassurance, more empathy and understanding, more help doing daily activities, etc. Your partner may wish to talk about his or her depression, guilt, or anxiety much more than you feel able to manage.

> Alan: Julie wants me to talk with her all of the time about her depression, and it is such a downer. I mean, I care about her but I'm not a shrink and I feel like that's what she wants me to be instead of a husband. I would never tell her what a turnoff it is to me because that would hurt her too much. It's hard enough having to be superdad when she's out of it. Now I'm supposed to want to talk all of the time too?

YOUR ROLE

It's possible that your behavior is causing or contributing to your partner's depression because of your own needs for security and familiarity. Thus, you may unconsciously feel more comfortable when your partner is weak than when he or she is strong. This would be true if you grew up with depressed or needy parents, or you feel most at home around people who are suffering or needy in some way. You may be unconsciously motivated to contribute to your partner's depression because it feels more familiar to you than his or her happiness or health.

You may also feel pulled to do this if you grew up in a chaotic and rejecting household and feel less threatened by a partner with obvious flaws than one who is healthy, strong, and independent. You could feel more reassured knowing your partner is tethered to you with insecurities, rather than free to come or go as he or she pleases. I have worked with many couples where one spouse subtly or overtly undermines and shames the other and then complains about how depressed, tearful, and sensitive he or she is. Often the critical, undermining partner has an unconscious motivation to keep the other partner off balance as a way to elevate his or her status or security in the marriage.

If your partner is telling you that you're causing his depression, it may be that he is failing to take responsibility for his own unresolved conflicts or emotions. A common symptom of depression is to feel as if it's the other's fault. "If only you were more x, I wouldn't feel so y"—plug in the coordinates. However, it is important to consider that there may be a grain of truth to this accusation. The only way to evaluate this is to seriously address your partner's complaints for at least six months to a year and closely watch to see if he or she becomes less depressed as a result. You may also need to seek individual or couple's counseling to become aware of how you are or aren't contributing, or to gain additional support in living with a spouse by whom you feel burdened.

Recovering from depression for women is often achieved by learning to become more assertive and self-interested (Gilligan 1982). While this is also true for some men, most need to work less on entitlement and more on revealing fear, vulnerability, and the memory and effect of childhood hurt or trauma. Many men resist counseling because of the implication that they can't solve their own problems. If this is the case, tell your husband that you want him to go to therapy with you to help you learn how to be with him.

Tell him that you're obviously not doing a good job at making him happy (not that it *is* your job) and you need help learning what to do differently. This may mean that you'll go by yourself if he refuses.

STRATEGIES FOR LIVING WITH A DEPRESSED PARTNER

Take care of yourself

In marriage, it's easy to believe that making yourself happy takes something away from your partner or the family. Your depressed partner may also collude in your maintaining this belief. Fight against this by developing a daily/weekly routine of self-care and self-nurturance that makes your life rewarding.

Avoid being critical

"I'm so sick and tired of being stuck inside with you all of the time because you never want to do anything. Just because you're depressed doesn't mean I don't get to have a life. You are such a drag to be around. I can't believe I'm married to you." Use empathy instead. It's better for you, and it will decrease the likelihood of conflict between you: "I'm sorry you don't feel like going out again this weekend. I don't feel like staying in though, so I'm going to go out with our friends anyway. Let me know if you need anything while I'm out." If your partner objects, don't escalate into blame as a way to manage your guilt. Remain empathic and stick to your goal. "I know you really want me to stay, but I need to see my friends."

When you do have complaints, try to put them in a way that doesn't sound like a criticism. Say something like, "I feel a little unappreciated. I made a nice dinner and cleaned up and you just went upstairs without even a thank-you. It would mean a lot to me if you acknowledged how hard I've been working." This is better than saying, "You know, you just sit on your fat ass and I do everything and then you go upstairs like you're the fucking king of the castle. Well, screw you, I don't have to put up with this shit!"

Use "I" statements when voicing complaints. "I" statements emphasize your reactions rather than the other's character. Some examples are:

"I am interested in your feelings, but when you say it like that, it makes me feel like a terrible person."

"I know you're having a hard time and I'd like to help. It means a lot to me when you tell me your feelings in a way that isn't a put-down."

"I have been reaching out to you and each time I get pushed away. I end up feeling like I'm trying harder than I'm comfortable with."

Find compromises

Let your partner know that you are aware that he or she is unable or unwilling to be with you in a way that you would prefer. Find a win/win approach. For example, try saying, "Okay, I know you hate to have people over, but I like it, so we have to find some middle ground that works for both of us." Start with what you would like, ideally, and then move to a compromise. "If it was up to me, we'd do something with friends every weekend." Get your partner to state his ideal. If you know what it is, have him state it anyway, to reinforce that this is a negotiation. "I understand that you don't like people over at all. How about every other weekend?" If your partner refuses your reasonable attempts at compromise, then you have to be more assertive. "Right now we're doing it your way, and that's not fair to me. I know it takes energy for you to socialize, but we have to come to an arrangement that works for both of us. You can choose not to come downstairs or be here, but I want to be able to have my friends come over."

Don't infantilize

It's tempting to give up and take over if your partner suffers from depression. However, most of the time, that isn't a good idea. While you may have to adjust your expectations downward, you are right to expect your spouse to make some efforts at partnership. However, as in any conflict, you'll get a better response if you communicate it without criticism. It's tempting to say, "Get off your ass and do something for once. Just because you're depressed doesn't mean that you don't have to do anything." Or, in passive-aggressive mode, "I have to do everything around here, as usual." But be direct instead: "I know you've been feeling bad, but I need more help. Here's a list of what we need to take care of over the next month. What can you agree to do?"

Know your limits

As a spouse, there are *absolute limits to how much you can do to help with a partner's depression.* It's good to strive to be empathic and helpful, but you're not a therapist and you can't run your partner's life. Avoid overinvolvement: "I think you'd feel a lot better if you called up a friend or went to the gym. You should also read that chapter in *Feeling Good* that Lisa was talking about. You can't just spend the whole night sitting around feeling sorry for yourself. What are you going to do today?" While this could be experienced as affectionate on the part of your partner, it could also feel intrusive, patronizing, and guilt-inducing.

As we saw in the prior chapter, blame and anger are unconscious attempts to rid yourself of feelings of worry, responsibility, and guilt. They are ways to say, "I'm not the bad spouse, you're the bad spouse!" In doing this, you temporarily feel relieved of the guilt of being unable to make your partner happy. However, blame and anger perpetuate the cycle of bad feeling between the two of you and lead to an escalation in conflict or depression.

Offer help

Knowing your limits doesn't mean that you can't help or ask your partner if he or she would like help. "Do you need anything before I go out? Can I do anything to make you feel better?" If the request is something that you can reasonably do *without resentment,* then do it. If you can't, let your partner know that, without blame or criticism. The depression may make it hard for your partner to let you help him or her (Rosen and Amador 1996). This is because of the guilt and underlying feelings of undeservedness and hopelessness that characterize depression.

Get support

Don't catastrophize that you're married to someone who's not more available. Your spouse may not be able to do anything about his depression, or he may be unwilling to. You can't waste precious years bemoaning what you're not getting from your partner. Learn to be your own best friend. This can be through spending time alone doing what you love or doing things with people you enjoy.

CONCLUSION

YOU MAY HAVE to accept that your partner doesn't and won't have a lot to give. This may be because he or she is depressed, or is in some other way unable to be the kind of partner that you'd like. If you have worked hard in the ways that I am suggesting in this and other chapters, you have to adopt a different stance in your marriage, a stance of acceptance. On the other hand, if you suffer from depression, your view of your marriage and the rest of your life may seem more hopeless and unworkable than it really is. Getting therapy, medications, or support may empower you to make your marriage more meaningful and gratifying. You may become more in touch with whatever initially drew you to your partner. Or it will give you the strength and energy to achieve happiness regardless of your feelings about your partner.

One of the hallmarks of depression is an inability to experience pleasure. This almost always translates into the sexual and romantic realms. While depression can reduce sexual desire, problems in marriage often translate into problems with sex. This is where we turn next.

6

———————————

Sex

Intimacy, distance, and affairs

"I'm so pissed off at him most of the time, I don't want him anywhere near me. The last thing on my mind at the end of the day is having sex!"

—NANCY, AGE THIRTY

"We haven't made love in months. I just don't think she's that into sex and I'm going crazy over it. She says she wants to feel more connected first, but how am I supposed to feel connected if we never make love. I guess this is what they mean by a loveless marriage."

—WALTER, AGE FORTY-TWO

CLAIRE WAS A forty-two-year-old woman who worked as an architect for a San Francisco firm. She had been married to her current husband, David, for twelve years and had a four-year-old son with him and and a sixteen-year-old daughter from a prior marriage. In our initial meetings she made it clear that because of her children, she didn't want to leave her marriage. She said that she needed help understanding how to stay married when she felt so little sexual or romantic interest in her husband.

Interactions around sex can provide some of the most intensely pleasurable feelings and some of the most frustrating and humiliating. Sex in the difficult marriage is one of the first things to go and often the last to return, if it returns at all. Because sex can be such an important part of our identity and potential pleasure, this chapter will address the nature of sexual difficulties, the different meaning of sex for men and women, the relationship it has to our identity, and whether you should strive to have a better sexual relationship with your partner. We'll look at ways you can begin building or rebuilding that part of your marriage and look at what to do if that isn't possible or desirable. The second half of the chapter will discuss why affairs are common and discuss what to do if your marriage has been affected by them, or if you are having an affair.

I'M NOT IN THE MOOD

A DECREASE IN SEXUAL or romantic desire is common in most marriages. However, sometimes a decrease of sexual feeling or interest can stem from inner conflicts or problems in the relationship. The *absence of desire,* described by Claire, is one of the more common sexual and intimacy problems in long-term relationships (Schnarch 1998) and almost always occurs in at least one of the partners in a strained marriage. Sexual problems such as an absence of desire commonly stem from:

- a fear of hurting others
- a fear of being hurt
- feelings of guilt, shame, or self-criticism
- a fear of being controlled
- alcohol or drugs
- anger
- depression and anxiety
- medical problems
- stress and exhaustion

FEAR OF HURTING OTHERS

Arousal requires the ability to be both empathic and self-interested (Bader 2002; Weiss 1986; Weiss and Sampson 1993). Without empathy, sex becomes mechanical. Empathy is the way that you tune in to your partner's experience and feel what he or she feels. However, without self-interest, you're unable to be sufficiently self-involved to experience feelings of pleasure and desire. That is, if you're so preoccupied or worried about hurting your partner that you don't relax, you can't get turned on.

Claire confessed in our first few sessions that her worst nightmare was becoming a "castrating bitch" like her mother. She described her mother as "definitely not your loving stay-at-home mom that you hear about all of the time. No, mine was the 'I didn't get to have a good life so why should you' type." She said that her mother had received a scholarship to a prestigious art school when she was young but her father forbade her from going there and pushed her into getting married and having children instead. "I guess I have some compassion for her, but I don't really like her. She's a pretty embittered woman, and my dad and I got the worst of it. He was pretty shy and passive. He couldn't defend himself from her, let alone defend me."

People often strive to be better parents and spouses than their own parents.[1] Claire was aware that her father was hurt by her mother's control and criticism. As a result, Claire adopted a care-taking role with her husband in the early years of her marriage. This caused her to avoid telling David what she needed sexually or romantically for fear of hurting his feelings. She had developed powerful beliefs as a result of interactions with her mother, which left her believing that women, left to their own devices, are cruel and toxic and men are weak and can't defend themselves. She felt inhibited being passionate in bed because she thought her intensity would scare or intimidate him.

Claire gradually became hostile and contemptuous toward her husband as her marriage proceeded over the years. In our sessions, she rationalized this by saying that she couldn't control her feelings because she was "fed up having a child for a husband and wanted a man instead." Like many people, Claire married in her twenties someone who was different from whom she might choose now that she's in middle age. In David, she chose a partner who was safe, nonjudgmental, and familiar, like her father. While she could have chosen a man who was stronger and more confident when she was young, she didn't, probably because it would have exposed her to the dangers of being rejected as she had been with her mother. Choosing a man who was "weaker" than her allowed her to be in the safer role of potential rejector rather than the one who could be rejected.

In the second month of therapy, Claire revealed that she had been in an affair for the past four months. She stated that the sex in her affair was great because she didn't worry about hurting her lover. She described him as an egocentric prick, "but as sick as that sounds, that's partly what turns me on about him." Her worry about hurting her husband and fear of being critical like her mother meant she could relax enough to get turned on only when she was with someone she couldn't hurt. She ended the affair several months later. While she didn't want to disclose the affair to her husband, she believed she could take what she had learned from it and use it to better understand herself and maybe better her marriage.

I referred David and Claire to couple's therapy because I knew they would both need help navigating this difficult terrain. David would need advice about how to stand up to Claire in a way that was comfortable for him and reassuring to her, and Claire would need help with her feelings of contempt and the anxieties that underlay them. I suggested that, going forward, I continue my work with Claire individually and that David seek individual counseling in addition to the marital counseling.

When I work with couples or individuals with serious marital problems, I evaluate whether they can turn their marriage into something more fulfilling or whether they have to accept the real limitations of their relationship and work toward a more imperfect harmony. At this early point in the therapy, David and Claire's marriage and sex life have the chance of becoming more vital, if David can get stronger. He will be better able to achieve this if Claire gets control over her rages at him. People change under conditions of safety, not when they're under attack.

IMPERFECT HARMONY

For now, the jury is out on Claire and David. The legions of marital self-help books are founded on the premise that the reader is going to be willing to do the work to create change in the household. However, many don't, or for whatever reason, can't. Claire's creating the conditions of change will be necessary but not sufficient for David to change. David needs to work through whatever fears or anxieties he has that cause him to be passive and withdrawn in the face of Claire's anger. He has to be willing to be the kind of man that is strong enough to interest her, to move from the role of being a compliant son in the marriage to a compelling man.

Kierkegaard (1959 [1843]) wrote that you should "rotate the self" rather than leave the circumstance that's causing your discomfort. This analogy is borrowed from rotating crops as a way to prevent them from depleting or taxing the soil. Many people go from relationship to relationship as a way to avoid dealing with aspects of themselves that they find uncomfortable. While Claire or David could toss the dice and see what they get in a new relationship (kid complications aside), they would likely still be left with the same inner landscape that they want to avoid. Failing to deal with the psychological issues that one brings to a marriage is another reason why remarriages have such a high failure rate.[2]

WOMEN, MEN, AND SEX

The way that Claire got into her marital dilemma is not unusual. Women in our culture, and in most others, are socialized to be caretaking and self-denying. As a result, many have a harder time being appropriately self-interested in marriage and in lovemaking.

They worry about the well-being of a partner so much that they can't relax or be appropriately directive (Bader 2002; Barbach 1984, 1976). While some men's sexual abilities are also negatively affected by being overly worried about hurting a partner, they are nonetheless supported by a culture that encourages and rewards their self-interest.

It wasn't that long ago that many women were far less aware how to achieve orgasm or know what aroused them (Berman and Berman 2001; Barbach 1984). In the late 1940s and the 1950s, the Kinsey Report caused controversy when it revealed that women were as capable of orgasm as men. Many of the older women interviewed *never* reached orgasm during intercourse because they were born in the end of the nineteenth century, when women in Western societies weren't supposed even to be interested in sex (Berman and Berman 2001). Jennifer Berman, M.D., and Laura Berman, Ph.D., are codirectors of the Female Sexual Medical Center at UCLA and authors of *For Women Only*. They note that many women come to their clinic without a basic understanding of their sexual anatomy or knowledge of what their genitals look like. Many suffer from the belief that they're abnormal if they can't have an orgasm during intercourse, despite the fact that only 20 to 30 percent of the female population can (Berman and Berman 2001).

This is compounded by the reality that many men and women believe that men should know what to do in the sexual arena without direction (Barbach 1984). Some men feel humiliated by a wife's request for a different technique or approach because they take advice as a criticism, or complying with the request as an act of submission. In other words, rather than seeing sex as an interaction requiring approaches unique to each individual, they see it as an expression of their inadequacy as men. In addition, because men often obtain their information about sex from other men or from pornography (Barbach 1984), they're often wrong about what is exciting or gratifying to women. Sources of information such as pornography are especially problematic, as they're geared to a male's sexual fantasy, which typically is more graphic and orgasm-driven than women's sexual fantasies or desires (Bader 2002).

As psychoanalyst Michael Bader writes in *Arousal: The Secret Meaning of Sexual Fantasy,* male pornography is typically devoid of story or character development. "Such pornography has never been successfully marketed to women, whose porno or erotica has traditionally taken the form of romance novels where sex is subordinated to relationships and is usually marked by intrigue, innuendo, and seduction rather than direct sexual activity. The qualities of the hero's character is at least as important as his physique." He cites the research on cybersex by Alvin Cooper and colleagues which shows that women are more drawn to sexual chat rooms whereas men are far more likely to go to traditional pornography and video sites.

WOMEN, SEX, AND CHILDREN

Childbirth is a consistent cause of a decrease in sexual desire for women. It's common for women to experience a decrease or absence of desire while they're nursing and sometimes for months afterward. This is often due to the release of oxytocin, a hormone released during breast-feeding which is associated with feelings of calm and pleasure. Breast-feeding can cause problems with lubrication because it can suppress the production of estrogen and ovulation (Berman and Berman 2001). Anthropologist Sara Hrdy (1999) notes that this decrease in sexual desire likely evolved in women as a way to ensure that they wouldn't produce more children than they could care for. She writes in *Mother Nature: Maternal Instincts and How They Shape the Human Species:* "So far as the mother is concerned, the link between intensity of suckling and postpartum infertility prevents an organism already burdened by metabolizing for two from being saddled with another pregnancy and the even more daunting task of metabolizing for three." She cites tribes such as the !Kung of the Kalahari, where women have to travel great distances for food and water and can't count on help from other available women (allomothers). Women in those societies have far fewer children than those in societies where they have more help and travel shorter distances for food, such as the Hadza or the Ache' tribes.

It may be for these reasons that women's sexual drive appears to be more strongly affected by stress and fatigue than men's (Hrdy 1999; Kiecolt-Glaser and Newton 2001). Since in almost every culture women have primary responsibility for the care and well-being of children, stress and fatigue likely became wired to shut off a woman's sexual interest in order to make sure that she didn't get herself into a situation that would endanger her or her offspring.[3]

Men would have been less likely to evolve this connection because they could, in most cases, count on women to ensure the survival of their offspring. They could also ensure the survival of their children through multiple partners, something that women are much more compromised in achieving, given the amount of time and resources it takes to carry a pregnancy and care for a child. In addition, men aren't endangered by having to carry a pregnancy, deliver a child, or devote precious calories toward nursing a hungry infant.

Marital researcher John Gottman (1999) found that men who do the most housework have the best sex lives. This may be modern-day evidence of the age-old dynamic. Put in evolutionary language, a woman who perceives that her mate is invested in her comfort and security would be better able to relax and feel secure in her future safety and the safety of her children than a woman who experienced her husband as disinterested, unavailable, or selfish. Thus, she'd be more likely to want to become sexual with a partner who could help her and her offspring than one who wouldn't. Among other reasons, this may explain why male unemployment is such a strong cause for divorce for women (Hetherington 2002) and why women the world over are attracted to men who have resources (Fisher 1992).

Men's marital satisfaction is closely tied to sexual frequency and the absence of criticism, while sex is less a factor in women's overall marital happiness.[4] Because of these differences in gender, it's easy to understand why so many couples begin to have problems in the sexual arena once children come onto the scene. Husbands feel rejected by their wife's decrease in sexual interest and the wife's transfer of affection. Men have a harder time admitting to feelings of rejection and thus are more likely to respond with anger, criticism, or withdrawal from the marriage. They may retreat not only from the spouse but from the kids as well (Belsky et al. 1991). This is often a crisis point in marriages because each partner may look at the other, and wonder why they failed to see these unappealing qualities that now seem so apparent.

However, gender is only part of the picture when it comes to sexual satisfaction in marriage. Another key aspect is the way that the past affects who we are, and the beliefs that we bring to the marriage about sex and intimacy.

FEAR OF BEING HURT CAUSES YOU TO RETREAT FROM YOUR PARTNER

Freud said, "We are never so defenseless against suffering as when we love" (Freud 1918). The fear of being hurt can cause you to shut down sexually, have affairs, or create fights as a way to decrease the feelings of being in danger. A lack of sexual desire in marriage is common, in part, because of your partner's increasing importance to you (Schnarch 1998). This may cause you to hide who you are as an attempt to prevent alienation or criticism from your husband or wife. This is particularly true if you bring powerful feelings of fear of rejection, shame, or humiliation into the marriage. Sexual feelings are based on a desire to connect, while feelings of shame make you want to retreat and hide (Bader 2002).

An unresolved fear of abandonment can unduly strain a marriage with the insecure partner's anxiety, accusations, tests, control, and abuse. It can create what is feared the most. As cognitive psychologists Jeffrey Young and Janet Klosko write in *Reinventing Your Life,*

"There are a lot of things you can do to make good partners seem like abusers. You can twist the things they say so innocent remarks take on the cast of cuts and insults. You can set up tests that fail to convince you, even when your partner passes. You can accuse them of trying to hurt you when they are not. You can magnify their disloyalties and minimize their acts of love. Even when they truly treat you well, you can feel as though you are being abused." Thus, a fear of abandonment may cause you to turn away a potentially good marital partner, or contribute to driving him or her into the arms of another.

FEELINGS OF GUILT, SHAME, OR SELF-CRITICISM PREVENT YOU FROM TAKING PLEASURE IN YOUR BODY, OR ALLOWING YOUR SPOUSE TO TAKE PLEASURE IN YOU

There are many situations that would cause this dynamic. You may have been raised by parents or in a culture that caused you to believe that sex is sinful or bad. You were raised in a family that left you feeling undeserving of love or attention. If this was the case, you may feel undeserving of your spouse's passionate interest in you. You might push your partner away in the same way that you felt pushed away by your parents. In addition, you may feel critical of your body and believe yourself to be too fat or too thin, or that your breasts are too saggy or your penis is too small. Self-criticism of one's body is a huge sexual inhibitor. This is especially true if your partner is also critical of your body.

FEAR OF BEING CONTROLLED CAUSES YOU TO FEEL TRAPPED AND SMOTHERED BY SEX

Because you are afraid of being controlled, you have a hard time relaxing during lovemaking. You experience your partner's desires to be close as an attempt to take you over, intrude upon you, or use you. As a result, you may experience little interest in sex, or you experience an uncomfortable degree of anxiety during it. On the other hand, a fear of being controlled may cause you to be excessively controlling during sex. It may make you insensitive to your partner's requests out of a fear that you will have to give up too much of yourself.

Parents who are controlling and perfectionistic sometimes create children who grow up to be submissive in marriage. They don't feel entitled to assert themselves in marriage and end up feeling trapped, resentful, and neglected. This may cause them to avoid communicating what turns them on or off. Others may have affairs as a way to feel less under the control and influence of a spouse.

> Jennifer: My father was a sergeant in the Marine Corps and he ran our house by yelling out orders and expecting everybody to jump. He reminds me of the military father in *American Beauty*. My mother felt trapped in her life with him and took it out on me and my older brother. My husband is a control freak just like my dad. Ten years into the marriage, it's really gotten old. I've come to really hate him for it. I started having a thing with a guy at work because I needed some part of my life that was just for me.

Jennifer submitted to her husband because she didn't know how to be her own person in her marriage. She hadn't learned how to talk about her feelings or needs and hadn't developed a capacity to be assertive enough to see if she could get her husband to behave better. She shut down on her sexual feelings toward him as a way to feel separate from him and less under his control.

You Can Only Enjoy Sex or Have Sex When You're Under the Influence of Alcohol or Drugs

It's no coincidence that advertisements for alcohol invariably show someone in the act of seduction. In the short term, drugs and alcohol serve the purpose of shutting down the part of the mind that's connected to guilt, self-criticism, fear, and inhibition. Part of the appeal of substances is their disinhibiting properties. However, if abused over the long term, they gradually interfere with the ability to maintain sexual interest and performance.

LONELINESS

Loneliness is one of the more common reasons given by many women for their affairs (Spring 1997). Long-standing difficulties in resolving conflicts can make couples fail to take the day-to-day initiatives to communicate and connect. This can cause one or both members to feel lonely and isolated. Many people who grow up in homes with distant or removed parents carry deep feelings of loneliness throughout their lives. They bring these feelings into marriage, making it hard for their husbands or wives to be intimate with them. These feelings of loneliness may cause them to be mistrustful or suspicious of their partner's attempts to be intimate, sexually or emotionally.

FEELINGS OF ANGER AT YOUR PARTNER PREVENT YOU FROM BEING SEXUAL

Long-standing feelings of anger interfere with the desire to be sexually intimate. On the other hand, people sometimes maintain a stance of anger as a way to maintain distance they would feel unentitled to achieve without the anger. Remaining angry may be a way to justify avoiding closeness with your partner, sexual or otherwise.

DEPRESSION AND ANXIETY MAKE IT TOO DIFFICULT TO RELAX OR EXPERIENCE PLEASURE

The hallmark of depression, according to the *Diagnostic and Statistical Manual of Mental Disorders*, is an inability to take pleasure in life. This may cause you to be uninterested in sex or to lack the energy to perform adequately. Anxiety also makes it difficult to become aroused because it interferes with the ability to relax.

FEELINGS OF WORRY AND OVERESPONSIBILITY FOR YOUR SPOUSE CAN MAKE SEX FEEL UNAPPEALING

Worry about a spouse can make it harder to take pleasure in him or her. Worry creates feelings of guilt, protectiveness, or concern that sometimes are in opposition to what one needs to become aroused.

> Ryan was the only child of a single mother in northern Chicago. His mother was chronically ill and depended on Ryan to do everything for her. When Ryan became a teenager, he was prevented from dating because of his worries of leaving his mother, and her shaming him when he did. In college, he married a woman who was depressed and dependent, much like his mother. Over time, Ryan felt trapped with feelings of responsibility, guilt, and worry over his wife in the same way that he had with his mother. He hadn't developed the capacity to feel separate from others' feelings. Thus, when his wife was sad, he felt pulled down by it and obligated to cheer her up or solve her problems. This made him feel both angry at her and burdened by her. He sexually withdrew from her early in the marriage. Shortly after the birth of their second child, Ryan started an affair with his secretary. He contemplated leaving his wife because his lover made him feel so happy—if only his wife were more like his secretary. However, Ryan could experience happiness because he wasn't emotionally responsible for his secretary. If he ended up marrying her, he would eventually experience the return of his feelings of worry, guilt, and responsibility because those feelings were so unresolved inside of him.

This is why rotating partners so often fails. If Ryan was going to stay married for the sake of his children, he would need to learn how to feel less responsible for his wife's depression. He would need to gain much greater control over how much his life was being affected by strong feelings of guilt and worry.

MEDICAL PROBLEMS

As Berman and Berman (2001) point out, problems with sexual desire or performance can have a medical basis. Genital surgery can affect the sensory nerves of the labia and minor branches of the clitoris, making it difficult to become aroused or have an orgasm. In addition, any major pelvic surgery has the potential to damage the nerves and blood vessels leading to the vagina, uterus, and clitoris. If this happens, the blood flow through the arteries may be diminished, leading to a loss of sexual sensation and a decreased ability to become sexually aroused.

Sexual problems may have other bases. Coronary heart disease and high blood pressure can cause problems with vaginal lubrication, pain, and decreased pelvic and genital blood flow. Disorders of the adrenals, pituitary, and hypothalamus can also negatively impact sexual function.

Ninety percent of male impotence has physiological roots. These can stem from heart disease, excessive alcohol or tobacco use, diabetes, high cholesterol, medications, surgeries, and hypertension. By age sixty-five, about one quarter of all men have difficulty getting or maintaining an erection. This also occurs less frequently in men who exercise regularly. Aging causes a decrease in testosterone in both women and men. Low testosterone in men causes them to think less about sex and take longer to recharge after lovemaking (Masters et al. 1994).

PROTECTING THE KIDS

If you are living in a marriage that is without warmth or physical comfort, take care not to sexualize or overexcite your relationship with your children. Parents who are lonely are more vulnerable to leaning on their children to do what the spouse can't or won't provide such as affection, attention, or companionship.

> Matt: My mother never molested me but the way she touched me used to really creep me out. She'd rub my back or my neck but it wasn't like a mother, it's like I was her lover or something. I used to hate it and it took me a long time before I didn't feel weird when I started having sex!

It is equally critical that you refrain from complaining to your children about your partner's lack of involvement, interest, or availability, sexual or otherwise. Children are exquisitely sensitive to these needs in their parents and may accommodate themselves in ways that aren't in their best interest. They may feel pulled to be more flattering or interested in you than they should, because they hear about or witness your lack of fulfillment. If you frequently complain about the other parent you increase your child's vulnerability to depression and anxiety disorders, as well (Grych and Fincham 1990).

I don't say this to make you worried about being affectionate with your children. Children benefit from parents who are physically affectionate and who love spending time with them. Affection makes them feel cared about and comfortable in their bodies. I raise this issue to help you stay tuned in to your child's response to you. If your child seems overly worried about you and spends a lot of time wondering if you're okay, trying to behave in a reassuring or flattering manner, or otherwise adopting a role that seems out of sync for his age, he may need more reassurance that you don't need him to fulfill those parts that are missing in your marriage. This doesn't *always* mean that your child is behaving in a reassuring way in reaction to your behavior; some children's personalities incline toward worrying and caretaking. However, you should determine if your behavior is in some way eliciting this response.

Revitalizing Your Sex Life

If you have never been sexually attracted to your partner, you may never be. Nonetheless, if there are things that you believe *may* increase your attraction or restore a former attraction, it may be worth the risk to talk about your thoughts and feelings. If your partner has made requests that you have ignored, consider that you may be avoiding responsibility for the problems in your marriage by ignoring him or her. If you have become withdrawn and defiant as a way to express your disappointment or disapproval of your partner, you may be missing an opportunity to shift the dynamic in a more positive direction and revitalize your marriage.

I understand that if you're reading this book, love may be the last thing that you're feeling. However, unless you fall into the category of people who are 95 to 100 percent sure that there will never be any hope for their marriage, you should make a very serious effort to solve the sexual problems in your marriage. Sex is typically the first thing to go and the last to return in a long-term relationship. However, a small increase in sexual satisfaction can sometimes make a large difference in marital harmony. In addition, small changes and improvements in the relationship can sometimes increase sexual desire.

Begin a conversation about sex with your partner by expressing your love or positive feelings for him or her. Open the conversation by asking your partner what is pleasing or displeasing to him or her as a way to put you in the more vulnerable role first (Barbach 1984). Then state your own ideas about what's pleasing or displeasing. Be as specific as you can. "I would like it if we could talk more before sex, during sex, or afterward. I really like it when you play with my breasts like this, my penis like this," etc. State your needs and wishes clearly as requests, not demands. Put your requests in the positive: rather than saying, "You never want to have sex" or "You're so self-involved in bed," say, "I really like it when we make love. I'm wondering if you have any ideas about what I can do to have it feel better or more pleasurable for you." Write down what each of you thinks the other expects in terms of frequency. See if you can reach a compromise (Spring 1997). Assume it will be awkward to talk about, especially when you first begin to try (Barbach 1984).

Raise the topic of your sex life in a period of relative peace or harmony, never during a fight. If you raise this issue, be open to hearing your partner's complaints that aren't sexual in nature, such as a desire to have more time together, less criticism, more help with the house or kids. Work on the issues of shame, self-criticism, or embarrassment by listing your sexual anxieties with your partner. If your partner is trustworthy, tell him or her your worst fears. For example, "I'm worried I come too fast. I'm worried that you prefer women with bigger breasts. I'm too fat, I feel ugly without my clothes. I think my cock is too small." Agree to not make fun of the other's sensitivities.

Try to keep an open mind about what should happen sexually between you and be creative about satisfying each other's needs for closeness and sexual release. What matters most is not that you engage in any particular sexual act, but that you problem-solve as friends (Gottman 1999). Give cues during sex, for example, "Do it harder," "Yes, like that," or place your partner's hands where you want them.

Evaluate your inflated ideas about what sex should be like in marriage. Sex is almost never as passionate and dramatic as it is during courting. As Jeanette Winterson writes, "Sex in movies and magazines is often portrayed as a fiery furnace when in real life it's more like central heating with an irregular thermostat" (Winterson 1989 in Spring 1997).

Expect progress with sex in your marriage to go slowly. Use these guidelines on a regular basis. As Lonnie Barbach writes in *For Each Other,* "Very often an exercise is carried out only once or twice or a few exercises are carried out one time each and when immediate headway is not made the entire project is abandoned. From lack of motivation, ambivalence generated by fear of the unknown, and just plain inertia, the subject of the sexual exercises fades into the background and is not brought up again by either partner. Instead the sexual dissatisfaction smolders, coloring other aspects of the relationship. *It is often easier to endure the pain of an unsatisfactory relationship than the discomfort required to change it.*" (Italics added.)

Or you can also use the following eleven strategies to guarantee a bad sex life.

Eleven Strategies to Guarantee a Bad Sex Life

1. *Never go out on dates.*
2. *When you do go out on dates, talk about all of the problems that exist in your partner or your relationship.*
3. *Criticize your partner's body. Men, you'll find this especially effective if you'd like a bad sex life with your wife.*
4. *Bring up a conflict shortly before bed.*
5. *Bring up your sexual requests or complaints only during fights.*
6. *Negatively compare your partner out loud to your previous spouse or partners.*
7. *Expect your sex life to be like it was when you were dating or when you were eighteen.*
8. *Ignore or insensitively handle your partner's requests concerning what excites him or her.*
9. *Have your children sleep in the same bed as you or stay up so late that sex is guaranteed not to happen.*

10. *Don't work on your communication and affection in the rest of your marriage.*
11. *Don't prioritize your own needs, because that way you're guaranteed to be too exhausted and stressed out to make love.*

WHEN ALL ELSE FAILS

Author, sex therapist, and syndicated sex columnist Isadora Alman (2002) recommends that you take responsibility for and control over your needs for touch and caring. "If it's impossible to have any kind of a physical relationship with your partner, do whatever you can to enliven your fantasy life. Get oils, sex toys, erotica to make your solo experience as pleasurable as possible. Others find that even the warmth and comfort of a pet is helpful in feeling more physically soothed and less deprived. Some couples make a handshake deal around sex. 'I'll do you once a week or twice a month.' It may not be emotionally fulfilling or even intimate but it's sometimes enough to maintain the peace so they can keep the family together." Alman recommends other activities for sex- and touch-deprived partners, such as ballroom dancing, where you can have the experience of being held or touched in a nonsexual way. Getting massages is another way to gain physical comfort.

A small percentage of couples agree that they will tolerate affairs within limits such as only on business trips, or only with people outside of the social group. Alman notes that it's better if a couple can discuss this in an explicit way because they can decide what is acceptable and what is unacceptable to each. However, most couples aren't able to do this, and even mutually agreed-upon affairs can become problematic because of jealousy, or because one of the spouses becomes attached to a lover and wants a divorce.

AFFAIRS

"I'm in love with someone else but I don't want to leave my marriage till my kids are in college. My lover brings out parts of me that I never knew existed."
—KAREN, AGE FORTY-FOUR

"My spouse just takes and takes. Having an affair is the thing that keeps me in my marriage; otherwise, I'd go crazy."
—MIKE, AGE TWENTY-EIGHT

"My partner isn't that interested in sex and I can't live without it."
—CARLA, AGE THIRTY-TWO

There are probably as many reasons that people have affairs as there are reasons that couples have problems. In *The Good Divorce,* sociologist Constance Ahrons notes that it's not uncommon for someone to have an affair as an exit strategy from a marriage. This can be a way to force a separation and at the same time have someone to go to once the marriage ends. In other cases, people sometimes seek in their lovers what they lack in themselves, such as when a depressed man looks to identify with a lover's youth and vitality. They may seek in their lovers the same qualities that initially drew them to their husbands or wives, or look for qualities their spouse lacks that they've come to believe they need or can't live without.

Some have affairs to escape a painful aspect of themselves, such as fears of abandonment or entrapment, loneliness, anger, or narcissism. Psychoanalyst Ethel Person (1988) writes that "love often burns brightest and endures longest when there are obstacles standing in the way of the permanent consummation of the union. Such circumstances allow one to both surrender (in intense, albeit limited doses) and autonomy; a rare opportunity to have one's cake and eat it too." If an affair has affected your marriage, your happiness will depend on understanding your behavior, whether you were the hurt or the unfaithful partner.

Statistics vary widely regarding how many people have affairs. In the United States, a conservative estimate is that 1 member of every 2.7 couples has had an affair.⁵ While affairs were once thought to occur more frequently among men in the United States, affairs among young married women are beginning to outpace those of young married men (Lawson 1988 in Goltman 1999; Hetherington 2002). Annette Lawson believes that this rise has occurred as a result of massive numbers of women entering the workplace. As women feel more financially stable and more comfortable with their sexuality, they feel more comfortable taking the kind of liberties that men have taken throughout history.

Anthropologist Helen Fisher (1992) observes that while affairs are found in almost every culture, so too is the requirement of discretion. In the southern Italian towns along the Adriatic, long-standing affairs are common, though never discussed publicly. In contrast, the Kuikuru of Amazonia commonly have between four and twelve extra lovers at a time, and unlike the people of coastal Italy, enjoy discussing them in social settings. However, here as well, husband and wife refrain from speaking of their outside sexual adventures with each other out of a desire to protect the family bond from the disruptions of jealousy.

In my practice, I have witnessed how affairs can ruin a marriage and hurt the children who were dragged through them. I have also seen them serve as a corrective wake-up call to a couple where one or both members refused to acknowledge the seriousness of their difficulties. In addition, I have worked with people who wanted to stay married and chose to have a short- or long-term affair as a way to meet desires that, rightly or wrongly, seemed impossible to meet with a spouse.

IF YOUR PARTNER IS HAVING AN AFFAIR

Gender differences sometimes show up in how men and women handle the discovery of an affair. When men are asked why they have affairs, they often respond that it was primarily out of curiosity, desire for risk or excitement, or because they felt sexually unsatisfied in their marriages. Men are more likely to assume that their wives had an affair for the same reason that they would. Thus, a man may assume that his wife's fooling around is because he's not good in bed: he comes too fast or too slow, he's too small, too unimaginative, or too unmanly. As E. Mavis Hetherington (2002) writes, "Men are master compartmentalizers—a fact reflected in the number of males who had both high marital satisfaction and an occasional casual sexual encounter." Women's infidelities were usually driven by marital dissatisfaction. "When women had an affair, it was less likely to be a one-night stand and more likely to be a committed relationship that led to divorce."

Women often assume that their husbands are having affairs for the same reason that they would—a greater sense of connection and understanding (Spring 1997). When an affair is discovered or revealed, women more commonly get depressed and try to preserve the relationship with the spouse, while men are more likely to get angry and want out of the relationship. These are perhaps different strategies of managing feelings of humiliation, shame, jealousy, or rejection. Obviously, these gender differences speak to trends and aren't etched in stone.

If your partner reveals an affair, part of your task is to determine if he or she can be trusted again. One way to evaluate this is to analyze whether the affair is part of an overall pattern of deception or a more solitary incident. Is your spouse trustworthy in other areas of his or her life, or frequently deceptive? Does he or she suffer from untreated substance abuse, and if so, is he or she willing to get into recovery?

You also have to be willing to consider your own potential culpability. While no one ever *makes* anyone have an outside relation-ship, there may be factors in how you communicate or relate to your partner that increased that likelihood. Some people are more likely to have affairs when their spouses behave in ways that are overly possessive, self-centered, critical, or rejecting. These behav-iors might make a spouse desperate for attention, nurturance, or concern—behaviors that are in ready supply during an affair. Understanding how you may have contributed to your partner's af-fair will be useful for strengthening your marriage and for exam-ining aspects of yourself that need strengthening.

If there is reason to believe that your partner is sincere in the desire to change and expresses a willingness to do so, over time you may want to move toward forgiveness. Remaining angry can serve the useful function of keeping you on the lookout for future betrayals and sending a message that you won't be mistreated again. However, you pay a high price for it, and your children may suffer as a result. It's possible to be forgiving without wearing blinders.

Your ability to forgive will be aided by witnessing your partner's efforts to change. Therefore, try to be clear with your partner about what would make you feel the most secure and reassured. Read a self-help book together on affairs, such as Janis Abrahms Spring's *After the Affair* or Frank Pittman's *Private Lies*. (See References.) If you are unable to heal the damage of the affair, get additional help through individual or couple's counseling.

If You Are Having or Considering an Affair

Some of my clients have reported that an affair was helpful to them and either strengthened their marriage or allowed them to feel nur-tured in ways that their partner refused to. Their view is something like that voiced by anthropologist Mary Catherine Bateson (2001): "A couple is a partnership in the commitments of child-rearing, business, and meeting the wider society. These are common goals that must be honored in spite of wandering erotic or romantic impulses." Others report that having an affair was helpful in that it allowed them to learn something important about themselves and their marriage.

> Regina. My husband used to always criticize my body. "Your boobs are saggy. Your ass is so flat." I got so self-conscious and felt so bad about myself that I didn't want to ever have sex with him, which he wasn't pleased about. It wasn't until I had an affair with Eric, who loved my body, that I felt confident enough to tell my husband he needed to shut up about it and appreciate me or he wasn't going to have me as a wife. I never told him that I had an affair, but he got the message that he needed to treat me better to keep me around.

You may not be able to know whether you can have a fulfilling relationship with your husband or wife until you have done serious work on yourself and on your marriage in the ways detailed throughout this book. You may be having an affair, or considering one because you have prematurely given up on your partner owing to your own anxieties, insecurities, or unresolved childhood pain.

On the other hand, only you can decide the balance between gratification, fulfillment, struggle, and risk in your life and marriage. The purpose of this book is to help you make the best decisions possible for the sake of you and your children. If you have an affair, then you have to do it in a way that minimizes the potential harm to you and your family. If you're staying for the sake of the kids, then every decision has to be thought of in that context.

San Francisco family therapist and sex educator Melody Matthews Lowman (2002) has informal guidelines for her clients when they discuss their desire to begin or continue an affair. "Affairs can destroy a marriage. I prefer to help people get their needs met within the marriage or find less problematic ways to find gratification. However, the reality is that people in the United States talk monogamy, but outside relationships are common. Because the individual is choosing to engage in a non–socially acceptable relationship, it is inevitable that they will feel conflicts of conscience which could lead them to use poor judgment, both in whom they have an affair with and whom they talk to about it."

"I recommend that individuals who are having affairs be explicit with a lover about the terms of the relationship so there are a minimum of misunderstandings. The worst problems come about when there's a disparity of interest between the two people that isn't being discussed. Then you have a lover calling up somebody's wife or husband trying to break up their marriage."

Lowman has observed that individuals who accept that the outside relationship has limits are the most likely to protect a marriage and children from the harm of a discovery. These parameters include the use of safe sex, the agreement to not call the other at home, and an acceptance of the inability to spend birthdays or holidays together. She states that the selection of the partner has to be sensitive to the children as well. If the partner is a child's teacher or the parent of a child's friend, then the child is more at risk if the affair is discovered or revealed. In other words, if you're staying for the sake of your children and you're having or considering an affair, then you have to be able to protect your children from its potential harm. However, even the most cautious are sometimes caught and have to deal with the painful consequences.

DISCLOSING AN AFFAIR

If you have had an affair and are considering revealing it to your spouse, you should be clear about your reasons and about the potential problems of doing so. While I don't encourage deception, honesty can sometimes cause more overall damage than maintaining silence. Philip Blumstein and Pepper Schwarz (1983) found that when husbands learn their wives' secrets, their marriages are likely to worsen or end in divorce. Another study showed that up to 40 percent of women and 30 percent of men said that their confessions did irreparable damage to their marriages (Lawson 1988).

Many people feel too hurt and betrayed by the news to trust a husband or wife again. If you're going to reveal your affair, you should understand that you may be putting your marriage at permanent risk. You should ask yourself if your partner is the kind of person who could integrate and grow with this information, or if he or she will feel too angry, hurt, or humiliated to recover. You should be aware that if you're doing it for the sake of relieving your guilt, it may not have that effect; your spouse may feel so betrayed that you will be unable to gain any closure on your feelings of guilt.

On the other hand, some find that disclosing an affair sometimes wakes up a partner to long-standing issues that have been ignored.

Belinda: My husband and I had a really bad marriage for eighteen years. I was staying for the children and counting down the remaining years till I could get out. I ended up having an affair with an old friend and it was really nice; nice to be appreciated, nice to be touched in a loving way. Well, Frank got suspicious and asked me about it and I admitted to it. I'll be damned if he didn't get his act together overnight. He confessed that he'd been a selfish husband and said he really wanted to work to save the marriage. He's been a total sweetheart ever since. I had no idea he had it in him. I'm not proud of my fling but it sure got him to get his act together.

There may be other reasons to reveal an affair; it may help you to avoid straying in the future if it's out in the open. It may also help your partner to pay a little closer attention so that it doesn't happen again. In addition, if the underlying issues are addressed, it has the potential to reaffirm the priority of the marriage (Spring 1997).

While the person who has had the affair often feels enlarged by the experience, the other spouse typically feels diminished. If you're the unfaithful partner, it's up to you to do the lion's share of the work reestablishing trust and safety in the marriage. You should assume that your affair will take a long time to work through. Don't be impatient with your partner to resolve his or her feelings prematurely; an affair is almost always humiliating to the person who was hurt by it. You will need to do large and small shows of goodwill in order to show your willingness to heal the wound and move the marriage forward.

You should ask your spouse what you can do to restore trust. Some of these requests may be minor, such as communicate more, come home earlier, get into individual and couple's therapy, or let him or her know if you have any contact with your lover. Major shows of goodwill might be putting all of the assets into a joint account, moving the family to another town, or quitting the organization where the lover belongs, or where you're most likely to have contact with him or her (Spring 1997).

CONCLUSION

OUR FEELINGS AND IDEAS about sex contain a snapshot of our identity. Within it live our fantasies and our longings, our fears and our inhibitions. Sexual difficulties are more often the rule than the exception when marriage is challenging. Working through sexual difficulties requires an ability to take risks to discuss and explore what will make you feel safe, cared about, or excited. If you have given up on your marital sex life, it's critical that you manage your feelings in a way that doesn't create problems for your children.

Affairs are initiated and maintained for many reasons. If your partner has had an affair, you may still be reeling from the discovery. Your future serenity will depend on your ability to resolve your feelings in a way that is good for you and your kids. You'll have to determine if your partner is someone who is capable of your trust going forward, and understand how your behavior might have contributed to the occurrence of the affair. If you had or are having an affair, you may have concluded that your marriage is incapable of providing you with what you desperately need to feel cared for or alive. While this may be true, it could also mean that you have prematurely given up on your partner and avoided doing the hard work that everyone has to do to change their marriage.

7

The High-Conflict Marriage

Stay or leave?

"Gary is a big screamer. On a scale of one to ten, everything's a ten with him. If he's late for work, he's screaming. If he can't find something to eat, he screams. If the
kids disobey him, he screams. He's impossible to live
with."

—MARLA, AGE FORTY-ONE

"I get really tired of being yelled at and criticized all the
time by Maggie. It's always, 'You're so stupid, you're such
a jerk!' If it weren't for the kids, I would be out of there."

—NED, AGE THIRTY

DANA WAS A thirteen-year-old girl who was referred to my San
Francisco practice for psychotherapy. In our first meeting, she sat
down on my couch with her assemblage of backpack, Walkman,
Mountain Dew, and journal, and looked up briefly at me before she
looked back down to her hands. While she was only thirteen, her
dark eyes already showed traces of someone burdened by witnessing
too many battles.

When her pediatrician referred her to me, she said that Dana
likely suffered from depression due to problems in her family.
When I asked Dana if her doctor was correct, her eyes welled up
and she spoke very quietly, as if not to disturb someone in another
room. "My parents *are* kind of a problem. They're just always fighting. They scream at each other about something almost every day."

She paused, looking up at a tall plant in the corner and then back down. "It really sucks."

"That *does* suck," I said. "It's really hard to have that going on all of the time."

She nodded, playing with one of her many rings, as the tears ran down the side of her face onto her hands.

"Do they yell at you too?" I asked.

"Not really," she said quietly. "It's more like I'm the referee or something. Like they both want me on their side." She paused as if she wasn't sure if she was wading into forbidden territory.

"I could understand that," I offered. "Most kids don't want to have to choose which parent they're going to be close to."

"I don't want to be on anybody's side," she said. "They'll always say, 'Tell your mom to get her ass downstairs, tell your dad that I'm sick of his bullshit.' " She shook her head slowly, as if trying to rid the image from her mind. "I just want them to act like adults."

Dana was growing up in a home where her parents' daily, out-of-control shouting matches were making it hard for her to attend to her own life. Studies show that intense, ongoing conflict between parents creates psychological problems in children that can follow them into adulthood (Amato 2001; Amato and Booth 1997; Amato, Loomis, and Booth 1995; Cummings and Cummings 1988; Hanson 1999; Jekielek 1988; Morrison and Coiro 1999). Intense, ongoing fighting can make toddlers and infants so anxious that they have a harder time attaching to their parents (Cummings and Davies 1994). In older children and teens, such as Dana, severe and frequent conflict between parents often leads to disobedience, aggression, delinquency, depression, anxiety, and poor self-esteem in both boys and girls (Cummings and Davies 1994; Dadds et al. 1999). High-conflict marriages frequently cause children to become socially withdrawn and confused about social cues (Cummings and Davies 1994; Kelly 2000). Children who are blamed for the conflict fare the least well (Grych and Fincham 1990). Marriages like Dana's parents are tremendously in need of immediate intervention for the sake of the adults and the children living there.

EFFECTS ON PARENTING

HIGH-CONFLICT MARRIAGES directly interfere with the ability to parent. Recent studies show that fathers are more likely to withdraw from their children and from the parenting role in marriages that have constant fighting (see Doherty 1998; Pleck 1997). In addition, they may become more negative and intrusive with their children than fathers in satisfactory marriages or mothers in poor marriages (Belsky et al. 1991). Other studies reveal that the mother's feelings about the father can affect how much he stays involved with the kids and how much he enjoys being a dad. Angry mothers are more likely to try to exclude fathers from child involvement than mothers who aren't angry (Belsky et al. 1991). Both mothers and fathers are more likely to be depressed in a high-conflict marriage (Keitner and Miller 1990).

IS IT TIME TO LEAVE?

IF THERE IS any time when it makes sense to consider leaving your marriage, it's when there is ongoing, open hostility between you and your spouse. Children sometimes do better later in life if their parents divorce, if the divorce means an end to the hostile exchanges between the parents, *and* if they are then raised by a capable, involved parent. In that scenario, children may feel more protected by a divorce than remaining in a home with constant turmoil (Amato 2001; Amato and Booth 1997; Amato, Loomis, and Booth 1995; Hanson 1999; Hetherington 2002; Jekielek 1998; Morrison and Coiro 1999).

Unfortunately, divorce doesn't always mean an end to conflict. E. Mavis Hetherington (2002) found that 20–25 percent of high-conflict couples were still engaged in very troubled exchanges six years after the divorce. She writes, "The only childhood stress greater than two married parents who fight all of the time is having two divorced parents who fight all of the time."

STAYING MARRIED TO PROTECT A CHILD

SOME MOTHERS OR FATHERS decide to stay married because they worry about the effect of leaving their children unsupervised with the other parent in a divorce/shared-custody arrangement. While each person has to weigh the trade-offs, research shows that there may be wisdom in this. Having a healthy parent in the home can reduce the problems caused from being raised by a more troubled parent (Amato and Booth 1997; Laumann-Billings and Emery 2000; Neighbors, Forehand, and McVicar 1993). If the custodial parent has significant mental problems, this may lead to long-term emotional, social, and academic problems in the child.[1] Problems in the child occur because he or she doesn't have the healthier parent to confide in, to help him or her counter the damage of being blamed or shamed, or to use as a role model of how to deal with the troubled parent's behavior. In addition, children often feel more pulled to take care of parents with psychological problems, thus leaving less time for them to be children (Schwartzman 2002).

If a child feels supported by a parent, he is much more likely to maintain affectionate feelings for that parent later in life. He is also more likely to become socially involved in a way that is less likely in homes where children are deprived of both parents' support (Amato and Booth 1997). This is another reason why what might be healthy for the parent, leaving a troubled partner, can be hard on a child. It's also a reason why it's important to make sure that your unhappiness with your partner doesn't affect your parenting if you're staying together for your kids' sakes in a high-conflict home.

GOING FORWARD

THE FACT THAT YOUR SPOUSE, you, or both have been out of control doesn't necessarily mean that the story has to end there. It may be that changing how you respond to the conflict will shift the family in a way that's better for you, your children, *and* your marriage. Many of the problems that come from high-conflict homes can be greatly reduced when one or both of the parents learn to compromise and negotiate or when they are able to resolve some of their more significant conflicts (Cummings and Davies 1994).

The following section discusses living with a spouse who is verbally abusive. Dealing with a spouse who is *physically* abusive requires different strategies and therefore will be discussed separately, later in this chapter. However, there are many similarities in behavior and personality between verbal and physical abusers. Therefore, I recommend reading the whole chapter rather than skipping ahead. Both verbally and physically abusive spouses have some or all of the following characteristics. They

- are manipulative
- are loud and unpredictable
- have periods of out-of-control screaming or crying at you or the children
- may involve your friends or family members in the problems in your marriage in an embarrassing or provocative way
- constantly or frequently use shame, guilt trips, or humiliation as an attempt to get needs met
- use threatening or blackmailing behavior
- criticize and control sex, finances, or friends

- are possessive, jealous, and suspicious
- are insecure
- demand that you confront or end relationships with anyone who hurts, displeases, or offends them
- are critical or controlling around finances

WHY DO I PUT UP WITH IT?

THERE MAY BE LITTLE or nothing you can do to change your partner's behavior. However, if you haven't found a way to set limits on your verbally abusive partner, it may be because:

You have a fear of abandonment and are influenced by your need for approval and security.

You feel overly responsible for his/her behavior and well-being.

You are excessively worried about hurting your partner.

FEAR OF ABANDONMENT

It takes strength to live in a marriage and stay loyal to your own ideas, feelings, and needs. It may be that your fear of abandonment is so great that you have sacrificed your identity to avoid the anger and disapproval of your partner. The powerful desire to feel valued may be interfering with your ability to set limits on your partner's behavior, or it may interfere with your ability to pursue your own self-interested happiness.

If you are dominated by a need for approval, it is likely that you come from a home where some important aspect of you was belittled, denied, or squashed. You rely on validation because you are filled with a chronic sense of your own unworthiness. You live a minute-to-minute existence where approval temporarily disconfirms the painful feelings and beliefs you hold about yourself, while disapproval plunges you back into the experience of undeservedness. People who carry this belief can feel especially imprisoned by marriage.

> Antonia: I don't really think either of my parents cared that much about me. When they weren't fighting, which was almost never, they still treated me like shit. I don't know whether it was because they were alcoholics or if they were just really unhappy people, but I felt like I was this worthless thing that was just messing up their lives. Now I'm married to someone who's as self-centered and bullying as they were. And the problem is, I actually care what he thinks of me! He wouldn't hit me, but he can get pretty nasty.

While Antonia wasn't entirely financially dependent on her husband, she was terrified of losing him. This harkened back to her growing up feeling alone and unlovable. I told Antonia that I would be willing to work with her to try to strengthen her marriage. However, she wouldn't be happy with herself or her marriage until she stopped giving her husband so much power. We would have to get her strong enough to be able to face the possibility of his leaving her if she was going to decrease the stranglehold he had on her life.

It took Antonia six months to feel strong enough to talk to Marcus about changes she wanted to make in her life of which he disapproved. However, by the time she did, he was beginning to treat her better in response to her setting some limits on his behavior. Even though he was often still verbally abusive, for the first time he began apologizing, and he agreed to go to couple's therapy. Her home began to shift from being unbearable to a place where she had some control over her life.

Many women stay in marriages they might leave if they were financially able. Cross-cultural studies show that women who are the most financially secure are the most likely to leave their marriages if they're unhappy (Crittenden 2001; Fisher 1997; Hrdy

1999; Hetherington 2002). Conversely, women who are the most financially dependent are the most vulnerable to the negative financial effects of divorce. This leaves many frightened to adequately assert themselves in their marriages for their sake or, sometimes, the sake of their children (Crittenden 2001).

However, some women irrationally decide that they can't be assertive with a husband for financial reasons. They scare themselves out of doing the emotional work in their marriages that might force their partner to behave in a more respectful way. As psychologist Terrence Real writes in *How Can I Get Through to You?*, "I cannot tell you how many women I have seen who, over the years, tolerated their husbands' verbal abuse, unilateral decisions, wholesale withdrawal—only to find themselves in middle age dumped for younger women anyway. So much for the rewards of patience! Avoiding conflict may not be a safer choice in the long run, only a quieter one." Becoming assertive is key to your becoming happy, especially if you live with a partner who tries to run your life.

FEELING OVERLY RESPONSIBLE

Feeling overly responsible for a partner can make it harder to set appropriate limits on your partner's immature or out-of-control behavior. Tom, a carpenter, came from a home where he was consistently blamed and manipulated by his demanding father. His wife, Fiona, shared many of his father's blaming characteristics, and this caused a great deal of confusion and unhappiness in his marriage.

> Fiona is a major blamer and I really struggle with that. If we didn't have kids, I'd probably be gone. The other night she started screaming at me out of nowhere that it's all my fault she didn't get the raise she was hoping for. She said, "It's because of you! If I wasn't so stressed out by our marriage, I would've met my deadlines. I would be a helluva lot further along in my career if I was in a better relationship!" She started

throwing things, yelling at the top of her lungs. The kids were crying and everything. What a mess.

Tom grew up believing that he had caused his father's unhappiness. This left him vulnerable to irrational accusations from his wife that he was to blame for her unhappiness and for her poor behavior around the house with him and the children. He was drawn to someone he could take care of, like Fiona, because this was a familiar role for him, one he had taken on when he was young. As he became more in control and aware of his unconscious guilt, over the next several years of therapy, he was better able to calmly set limits on her behavior.

A partner's feeling overly responsible for the other's immaturity is a common dynamic in the verbally abusive household. This is because if someone is going to consistently lunge at her partner's throat, it's because she may be getting too much rope. Being able to set limits means being fairly clearheaded about your own rights, limits, and limitations. At the core of believing you're responsible are feelings of enormous self-blame, which get experienced as guilt, fear, or anxiety.

FEAR OF HURTING OTHERS

It's possible that you don't set adequate limits because you're afraid of your own strength or power to hurt others. Thus, you may be confused about the difference between being assertive and being abusive.

Nona grew up with a father who was depressed and withdrawn. She often observed him crying in response to arguments he had with her mother and repeatedly watched him submit to her out-of-control anger and criticism. As a result, she developed the belief that men are weak and should be protected. When she met Carl, a contractor, she was strongly attracted to his strength and charisma. "Even though Carl was critical of me from the outset, it didn't really bother me because I liked that he wasn't afraid to speak his mind. If he said, "That dress makes you look terrible," I liked that he was direct. I don't like men who tiptoe. I also felt like he cared enough about me to tell me what he really thought. Over the years, he's gotten meaner and meaner. I went from being the best lover in the world to constantly hearing about how uptight I am if I don't want to do some kinky thing he was into. And I'm no prude!"

Nona's fear of hurting others made her reluctant to confront Carl about his mistreatment of her. If you live with a verbally abusive spouse, then it is likely that you are confused about what you're feeling or what you're entitled to feel. You have become numb or learned to hide your anger or resentment because those feelings seem dangerous. You have forgotten how to feel pleasure or joy because guilt and resentment have become so consuming. You may have become ashamed or protective of your sexuality, and this has caused you to withdraw and shut down.

WHY DOES HE OR SHE HAVE TO ACT LIKE THAT?

VERBALLY ABUSIVE PARTNERS are rarely difficult in the beginning of a relationship (Forward 1997; Nelson 2001). More commonly they are charming and well controlled (Forward 1997; Nelson 2001; Walker 1984; Weitzman 2000).

Charna: When Don and I first met, wow, talk about intensity. I've never had so much excitement in my life! Everything was so fast; we were living together within six weeks and engaged one month after that. I remember saying, "Hey, slow down there, cowboy, what's the rush?" But after dating all of these men who had commitment problems, it was exciting to finally find someone who really wanted to get serious. I think because of that, I allowed him to set the pace and didn't set any limits. I ignored that little voice in my head that was saying something is a bit off with this guy. Even though I felt bothered that he didn't want me to spend time with my friends, I was also really flattered that he wanted me all to himself. I saw it as love, and maybe some of it was. But it was also a lot about his need for control. By the time we had a child, he was used to just running me over if I didn't want to do what he wanted.

Abusive spouses can often seem cruelly monochromatic when viewed through the unforgiving light of their spouse's experience. However, nothing is ever simple in human behavior, and this is true with spouses who are explosive, angry, exploitative, and aggressively controlling. However unsympathetic their behavior may be, they often come from homes where they were the victim of or witness to emotional or physical abuse (Walker 1984). They carry intense, unconscious feelings of shame, guilt, humiliation, neglect, sorrow, and anger that affect their feelings of safety and their ability to be intimate in marriage. While this is never an excuse for their abusive behavior, gaining empathy and understanding of them is a key step in becoming more independent of their power and influence over you.

Some partners learned to become abusive because they were raised in homes with too little structure, limits, or controls. Thus, they weren't taught the self-control that is necessary for everyday communication and intimacy.

Mel was raised in a large, poor family in rural Iowa. His father died when he was three and his mother never remarried. Because his mother was constantly depressed and overwhelmed, he had very little supervision or limits. He discovered at a young age that he could bully his mother into doing whatever he wanted, whether it was staying out late or giving him money, despite the fact that they were poor. He grew up feeling both neglected and powerful at the same time. When he got married to Jane, he continued this bullying behavior to get his needs met in the marriage.

MENTAL ILLNESS, ADDICTION, AND ALCOHOLISM

Your partner may be verbally abusive because he or she suffers from mental illness, alcoholism, or addiction. In most households, men are more likely to become angry when depressed, while women more commonly withdraw. Both men and women are more likely to lose control of their emotions if they suffer from mental disorders such as bipolar disorder (manic-depressive illness), paranoid schizophrenia, or many of the personality disorders such as borderline, histrionic, or paranoid personality. (See the *Diagnostic and Statistical Manual of Mental Disorders*, 4th ed. [2000].)

Regardless of the cause, you will likely need leverage if you are going to try to get a partner into therapy or treatment if there is addiction or mental illness involved. You should not try to reason with your partner when he or she is drinking or using drugs, as those are the times when people are the least in control of their emotions and behaviors. If they don't respond to the suggestions and strategies presented here and in the next two chapters, you will have to use whatever leverage you have to get them into treatment.

Identify your sources of leverage. Is it your respect? Time together? The marriage? Set up a hierarchy of consequences if he or she refuses to change, ending with leaving the marriage if it has come to that (Young and Klosko 1994). Be empathic with how hard it is to change but firm in your expectations. For some individuals, medication, recovery, or psychotherapy can make the difference between a workable marriage and one that is a living hell.

FEAR OF REJECTION

Many people who are verbally abusive are struggling against an enormous fear of rejection. They feel terrified of losing their partner and respond to those feelings with control, threats, and intimidation. Many abusers are surprised to learn that a husband or wife feels intimidated by their behavior because the abusers feel so weak, afraid, and inadequate inside. In addition, because they feel unworthy and unlovable, they have a hard time believing that their spouse would want to stay if he or she weren't being coerced. Often we repeat in marriage what we observed growing up. Thus, if your parents yelled at each other or you, you're more likely to yell at your spouse or your children. This was true of Bonnie.

> Both of my parents were out-of-control screamers. There was no middle range in my house. There was only screaming or silence. I would never put a child through what my parents put me through. You never knew when somebody was going to go off on you. Most of my childhood was spent in a state of shell shock.

However, while Bonnie might have been less abusive than her parents, she was still not in control of her behavior with her children. Her yelling at the children was one of the reasons that her husband, Noah, wanted them to start couple's therapy. He was concerned when their ten-year-old son began to have problems concentrating at school and his teacher recommended that he get therapy.

> Bonnie doesn't think she's a screamer, but she is completely out of control. And if I say anything then she'll just say how overreactive I'm being or how I'm pampering the kids. And she doesn't just scream at them or me. She screams at the cat, she screams if she drops something. She's even screamed at my parents when they asked her to talk a little more quietly. Whenever I talk with her about it she'll just say, "You're just too sensitive and you're making the kids that way, too."

It is not uncommon for people who grew up with rejecting or out-of-control parents to accuse their partners or children of being overly sensitive (Nelson 2001). Abusive spouses often come from homes where they had to deny their own vulnerability as children in order to feel less—less sadness, less guilt less anger, less loss. People like Bonnie who accuse others of being "too sensitive" are usually struggling to repress and deny their own sensitivity.

FEAR OF ENTRAPMENT

Behaving in an angry or rejecting manner is a common way to achieve distance in a marriage. Your partner may use anger as a way to feel separate from you because he or she doesn't know any other way of achieving it.

> Ari grew up in the United States with parents who had survived the Holocaust. His parents panicked if he was a few minutes late coming home from school and constantly feared that something terrible would happen to him. In addition, they depended on him for reassurance and support. As a result he grew up feeling burdened and trapped by their worry and needs. On the weekends, he was expected to work in the family business and help his parents in the evenings translating documents. He was forbidden to date until he was eighteen. Ari felt easily suffocated in relationships as an adult. In his marriage, he was filled with guilt when he wanted to spend time apart from his wife. He unconsciously believed that she felt as possessive and in need of him as his parents. The only way he could lessen his guilt enough to justify time to himself was to make her seem like a terrible person. So he constantly bullied and provoked her until she would storm away.

TESTING LIMITS

ABUSERS, WHETHER PHYSICAL or verbal, test their partners early on in a relationship to determine how much they can get away with (Forward 1987; Nelson 2001; Walker 1984). Often they come from homes where they didn't learn how to behave in a mature relationship, as we saw with Mel. They watched a father take advantage of a mother and a mother who couldn't object. There was alcoholism or drug addiction, or the adults were out of control in some other way.

Unconsciously, an angry or exploitative spouse wants to be reined in. He or she is out of control with you or the children because his or her emotions feel so unmanageable. Privately, he or she may feel like a terrible person for treating you or your children in a hurtful manner. Ironically, the way people sometimes reassure themselves that they're not ogres is to behave like ogres and hope that their partner can see through it (Weiss and Sampson 1986; Zeitlin 1991). Seeing through it, however, isn't saying, "I love you no matter how badly you treat me." It's saying, "You're not an ogre, so stop acting like one or I won't want to be around you."

LOOKING AT CHANGE

SETTING LIMITS doesn't mean that your partner won't fight your efforts. He will. And the longer you have tolerated him, the longer it may take to get him to change, if change is even possible. He may escalate mistreatment depending on how threatened he feels by your efforts. However, testing your limits is often an attempt to see if you can set those limits. If you didn't send a clear and consistent message from the beginning that certain behaviors were off-limits, your partner probably took that as permission to control or manipulate you in this fashion.

Submitting to your partner may make her feel more powerful in the short term. However, every time you give up and allow yourself to be mistreated, she loses more respect for you. She sees it as a sign of weakness that you give in, even if your giving in is an attempt to be caring or solicitous. You, like many people who live with an abusive or out-of-control partner, may believe that it's going to get better someday (Forward 1987; Nelson 2001; Walker 1984). Unfortunately, it will only get worse over time unless you begin working to change the dynamic.

Most if not all of the changes you are going to make may benefit your partner in the long run. While that's not necessarily a reason to do it, reminding yourself of this may help you push through the fear and guilt you have about changing. In the present situation, you feel controlled, criticized, dominated, suffocated, or used. This makes you less interested in spending time together or revealing yourself to your spouse in any meaningful way. It likely results in your not feeling sexual and may negatively influence your ability to be a good parent. It's possible that changing the dynamic in the household will put your marriage on a new footing that's better for everybody.

WHAT DO YOU NEED TO CHANGE IN YOU?

OVER TIME, YOUR MIND has played a trick on you, which allowed you to be banished to the corner of your life rather than stretching out and luxuriating in it. You, with your partner's pressure, began tolerating a threatening person who now has to be shown how to behave so that you and your kids can have access to the precious family resources of relaxation and safety.

While it is never your fault when your partner behaves poorly, you may have more responsibility for your home being out of control than you let yourself see. It's possible that you contribute to the volatile dynamic through your own behavior, such as subtle or overt provocation, passive-aggressiveness, manipulation, rejection, or shaming. If you grew up in an abusive or dysfunctional family, fighting may feel more familiar and predictable than peace and harmony. This may cause you to mistrust and sabotage periods of peace, or positive efforts by your spouse.

You may also unconsciously provoke your partner to anger so that you can have access to your own angry feelings without any of the cost or risk. This *projective identification* permits you to see the rage as something outside of yourself that you can control or criticize, rather than experience a feeling inside of you that you have repressed, or fear in yourself.

Finally, you may keep your partner angry as a way to justify your desire not to be close. This is because of your own conflicts about intimacy or because you have already decided that you don't want a more intimate marriage with your spouse. If this is the case, you might provoke your partner to behave badly as a way to feel more comfortable maintaining your distance. Again, while it's never an excuse for someone to be abusive, you may play a larger role in the dynamic than you're comfortable admitting.

YELLING AT THE CHILDREN

MANY, IF NOT MOST, parents yell at their children from time to time. Losing your temper sometimes is different from ongoing verbal abuse. While children feel hurt when their parents occasionally yell at them, it's unlikely that long-term damage is done if the overall relationship with the parent is sound (Ehrensaft 1997). However, if a large or primary aspect of interaction between parent and child is characterized by ongoing criticism, shaming, blaming, or yelling, then the other parent should find a way to intervene to protect the child.

Insanity can't run the family. If your partner's behavior is hurting your children, you can't allow him or her to be the stronger, more dominant voice. Staying together for the children's sake means changing whatever you have to change in yourself to be an effective and positive force in your kids' lives. If this pattern has gone on for a long time, you won't be able to turn things around quickly. It may take a very long time. You may also not be able to get your partner to change significantly. However, it is important that the children have a secure and close relationship with you, and that you are a good role model for them.

While it may be better overall for you to stay in your marriage, you have to help your children understand that the mean things that are being said to them are not true. They will need your help in detoxifying the effects of your partner's ongoing shaming or critical remarks. They may also need your protection in the moment when they are being criticized. This can be a touchy situation because, while you don't want to go behind your partner's back, he or she may be so out of control, so overreactive, or so uninsightful about the effect of his or her words that you have no other option other than to provide a protective barrier by speaking to your children after the fact.

Talking to the children about the other parent's behavior without that parent's consent is a last resort. First you should make sure that you've done everything in your power to help your partner see the effect of his or her behavior on your kids. To do this, you should ally with your spouse, refocus or reinterpret the children's behavior in a more positive light, and set limits, as I'll illustrate below. It's important that you don't use talking about the other parent as an opportunity to subtly align your children with you against the other parent. It may be dearly tempting if you feel abused, mistreated, or humiliated in the same way as your children. However, our role is to support our kids, not to have them support us. Failing to do this places them in a loyalty bind that is confusing and damaging. They still love their other parent, even when that parent is behaving poorly.

Sally's husband was alcoholic. When he wasn't drinking, he was a reasonable husband and father; however, he was a mean drunk. He would often say things to her and their two sons which were cruel and humiliating. Despite being an adequate father when sober, he rarely remembered what he said when

155

drunk, and wouldn't apologize to his wife or children about his behavior. If Sally confronted him for what he was saying to the children when he was drinking, he became more enraged.

I encouraged Sally to go to Al-Anon and to send her kids to Alateen. I also encouraged her to be honest and direct with her children about their father's behavior. "Daddy has a drinking problem. When he's drunk, he says things which I know hurt your feelings. These things aren't true about you and I don't think Daddy means them either. I'm trying to get Daddy help." I encouraged her to ask the kids what they thought or felt when their dad treated them in this way.

The purpose of this type of intervention is to help your kids understand that they're not being treated in a way that is reasonable or good for them. The following steps are designed to help you develop a strategy for protecting your children when your partner is being verbally abusive.

1. When your partner yells at the children, ally briefly with your partner *if the concern is just*, even if the communication isn't. If your wife is screaming at the kids to get ready for school, it's better to begin by briefly backing her up with words and behavior; "Okay, your mom said to get ready, so you guys need to speed it up." If your spouse's behavior often becomes abusive despite your stepping in, then you need to go to step 2.

2. Find a calm time to talk to your partner about his or her communication to the children in a way that isn't blaming, rejecting, or critical of the parenting. During this time, empathize with how stressed or worried or overwhelmed your partner must be. Parents almost always feel terrible about yelling at their children, even if they rationalize it by saying that the children need it, or that they're not harmed by it. Say something like, "Honey, you seem really stressed out and I'm worried about you. I'm wondering if there's any way I can be more supportive of you with the kids. Seems like they're really getting to you. I know they can be tough."

Several things may happen here. The first is that your spouse might use your empathy as an opportunity to blame or criticize *you* for his or her behavior; "Well, I've been telling you that I need you to keep this house clean and you know how enraged that makes me." The complaint should be addressed directly without your buying into the blame that sloppiness causes out-of-control marital responses. In that case you could say, "We can talk about that. Let's agree to what each of us wants in terms of cleanliness and come up with a compromise. I know that a cleaner house is really important to you." However, don't get sidetracked. Once you have that agreed to, return to the parenting. "So, how can I support you in those situations?"

Your partner then may use this as an opportunity to make observations about the children in a way that you know is wrong. "I just think we've been too lax on them and they don't know the meaning of the word 'respect.' It doesn't do any harm to them to let them know you mean business by raising your voice a little or taking a switch to their behinds. Joannie's eight going on eighteen. If she doesn't learn now who the boss is she'll never learn." Again, address the reality, if there's reality. "Yes, Joannie is a really tough kid and I really have to control myself not to yell at her, too. I know I'm far from perfect as a parent. I just want us to find some middle ground that feels good to both of us. I'd like us both to work on not yelling as much."

3. If you think your partner's assessment of your child is wrong, *reframe the criticism as an asset or value of the child.* "Yes, Joannie's very *spirited, energetic, ambitious,* and that sometimes makes her tougher to parent than the other kids. But I want to find a way to support you so that we can be calmer in our interactions with her." If your partner remains defensive, then you should move on to the next step.

4. Focus on your reactions: "*I'm* feeling stressed by what's happening at those times. You may be right that your yelling is not harmful to her. I don't know. In general, I don't think screaming at kids is great for them. My parents did it with me and I feel like

it's left its mark on me. But either way, it's hard on me when you yell at them, so I want us to have a game plan so I can step in or you can step back when it reaches a certain temperature. How about we agree that if I'm feeling uncomfortable with where it's heading, I'll step in and help in some way?"

"Oh, so you get to look like the good guy?"

"Absolutely not. I don't want to undermine your parenting in any way. I want the *two* of us to come up with a plan that feels good to both of us. Why don't we just track it together over the next month and brainstorm afterward."

If your partner agrees, be sure to reinforce him or her with appreciation. It is especially true if and when he or she begins to change the behavior toward more control. Be sure to notice and praise the times when your partner is doing a good job, especially when you see him or her struggling to maintain control. "I thought you did a beautiful job with Joannie today. You were really patient when she was being demanding." The more you appreciate and reward, the greater the likelihood of change. Conversations about parenting can be especially touchy, as all parents carry some feelings of guilt or inadequacy about it. Therefore, it's very important to be your most tactful and your most reinforcing.

There are often times when you should just step in between your children and your spouse and protect your children by saying something to the other parent like, "Okay, Joannie's got it. Stop criticizing! You don't have to put it like that" or "That's not appropriate! Don't talk like that!" or "Don't call them names! You can say what you have to say without using that kind of language!"

Each parent has to decide what he or she is willing to put up with in terms of the other parent's behavior. It may not be in anyone's best interest for you to intervene with every inappropriate comment or criticism your partner makes; you can't police everything that comes out of your spouse's mouth. On the other hand, you want to do it frequently enough so that your children have the experience and memory of your trying to intervene on their behalf.

If your partner won't agree to your recommendations and you're worried about the effect of his or her communication with the children, you should seek help from a couple's or individual therapist. You should also consider an evaluation from a child therapist. Sometimes difficult partners can hear and respond better to a professional than to the other parent. This can also be a good resource for you in terms of understanding how best to protect your child. I'll return to strategies for living in a high conflict marriage in the next chapter.

PHYSICAL ABUSE

LIVING IN A HOME with emotional volatility can be psychologically damaging, but living with a batterer may put your life in danger. It is especially in danger when you leave, threaten to leave, or seriously threaten the control your partner has over you, because batterers are the most likely to desperately increase their tactics at those times (Walker 1984; Weitzman 2000). While verbal abusers don't always progress to physical abuse, physical abusers are often verbally abusive, and share almost all of the characteristics listed earlier in the chapter. Physical abuse should always be taken seriously. There is a greater danger of physical abuse when a family is in a state of turmoil or change. Events such as a pregnancy, the loss of a job, moving, the death of a parent, physical illness, or a change in finances can precipitate violence (Walker 1984; Weitzman 2000).

While someone who is verbally abusive could become physically abusive, the best predictor of future violence is past violence, in or outside of the home, problems with impulse control, and a low level of guilt or remorse for hurting others. Many battered spouses carry the belief that it will get better some day. However, abusive behavior typically gets worse rather than better over time (Forward 1987; Nelson 2001; Walker 1984; Weitzman 2000).

More than 8 million couples a year engage in some form of

domestic violence. According to the largest and most recent survey by the United States Department of Justice, 39 percent of spousal assault victims are men, though they are typically subject to less violent forms of aggression than most women (Thompson 2002). Some people leave their abusive partners and feel liberated. However, if you have been in an abusive relationship, you're vulnerable to getting into another if you don't do serious soul-searching about whom you are attracted to. Getting married to your partner may have been terrible luck and there were no warning signs. More often, however, there are signals that get ignored.

Only you can decide what is in the best long-term interest of you and your children. Some parents stay with an abusive partner to protect their children from the other parent in a divorce/shared-custody arrangement; this may be because male batterers are twice as likely to seek sole custody in a divorce as nonviolent fathers, and 40–60 percent of them also abuse their children. (Walker 1984; Weitzman 2000). Helping professionals most frequently adopt the position that leaving is always the best option. This is understandable, based on the concern that their clients' lives may be in danger if they stay.

However, some people choose to stay and work on their marriage because it feels more empowering than leaving (Peled et al. 2000; Weitzman 2000). As social scientist Susan Weitzman (2000) writes, "Leaving is not the only option. I have learned that when I adopt the approach of exhorting a client to leave her abuser no matter what, I may lose the opportunity to work with her within the choices she is making. A basic social work tenet is to start where the client is and allow for self-determination. Besides, staying can feel empowering for some women. Perhaps the wife is taking steps to protect herself while she keeps her marriage intact. Others may stay as a part of secret strategizing. To think that leaving is the only solution can be arrogant or even disempowering. . . . For some, compromise may include staying married, but with new ground rules, or perhaps with a lower level of emotional commitment. I think a more important question than 'Can this marriage be saved?' is 'Can this *woman* be saved?' "

The following are some guidelines if you live with domestic violence:

- Call the National Domestic Violence/Abuse Hotline: (800) 799-SAFE (7233). Callers can be given immediate directions and assistance including emergency shelters, referrals, counseling, and reporting abuse.
- Web site: SAFE, Stop Abuse for Everyone <http://www.safe4all.org>. Comprehensive list of Web resources, local shelters, and personal stories of others who have lived with domestic violence. Useful for both women and men.
  Center for the Prevention of Sexual and Domestic Violence: Phone (206) 634-1903.
  National Coalition Against Domestic Violence: Phone (703) 765-0339.
- Develop a safety plan. This means that if you have to rush out of the door with your kids, you have a definite place that you can stay, with a person you trust. You should also leave changes of clothes there for you and your children, along with money.
- Assess your partner's willingness to change by suggesting he get into a batterer's intervention program.
- Begin with small changes in yourself such as slowly increasing your assertiveness and independence. The task is to develop yourself without acting or feeling like a victim in the marriage. Use the techniques recommended for working with verbal abuse, though you may need to go more slowly. Your safety is the top priority.

STEPFAMILIES

EVEN WHEN DIVORCE SUCCESSFULLY ends a high-conflict situation, marriages with stepchildren often bring their own sources of tension. Children can remain in conflict after a divorce, and well into remarriage. In addition, they may be consciously and unconsciously influenced by biological parents who still fight, inner conflicts about loyalty (even when the parents are allied), a parent who is no longer involved in their lives, stepparents and ex-spouses who are open in their dislike of each other or of the stepchildren, and psychological or temperamental problems in the child that preceded the divorce.[2] The fact that a high percentage of stepfamilies end in divorce may be testimony to the strain that combining families can pose. Stepfamilies also commonly disagree over financial issues such as giving or collecting child support and how money should be allocated to the children or stepchildren.[3] As a result of these tensions, many people find themselves in the difficult position of having to decide *again* whether to stay married for the sake of their children.

Stepparents

Studies show that stepmothers are much more likely to be demonized than stepfathers (Hetherington 2002; Visher and Visher 1979). Husbands often expect stepmothers to establish order in the household, and this is often resented by the children. As E. Mavis Hetherington (2002) writes, "Stepmothers are expected to be nurturers to already difficult and suspicious children. . . . In our most contentious stepfamilies, a real demonizing of the mother often occurred. Stepfathers rarely encountered this kind of vitriol. . . . Stepmothers had been able to build up the least closeness and goodwill with their stepchildren with less than 20% of young adults saying they felt close to their stepmothers."

In addition, stepmothers are more likely to feel depressed by the stepparenting experience. (Visher and Visher 1979). This is probably for the same reason that mothers feel more stress in *any* marriage—they're typically more worried, guilty, and involved in the lives of those around them. For example, a stepmother will be more stressed if she believes her new husband is neglecting his children, especially if she doesn't have the permission from the child or the father to parent. She may be caught in a no-win situation, with all of the guilt and none of the gratification. In many cases, it may mean that she'll do all of the work but receive none of the gratitude. In addition, the stepchildren may feel guilty toward their biological mothers for accepting the parenting.

Temperament of Stepchildren

For both boys and girls, the strains of divorce can increase problems in children who have difficult temperaments. Children who are more withdrawn or anxious, or more prone to act out in antisocial ways with aggression, defiance, or rule-breaking, may become even more at risk with a divorce (Ahrons 2002; Hetherington 2002). This is probably because these children respond to feelings of anxiety, sadness, guilt, or anger by striking out or by internalizing those feelings in a self-destructive way. Divorce has the potential to bring all of these emotions to the surface. While children with difficult temperaments can stress a nondivorced household, they doubly stress the household of the stepfamily. This is because the stepparent may feel both more burdened by the children's behavior and less invested in devoting the financial or emotional resources to helping the stepchildren (Hetherington 2002).

Strategies for Living Together in a Stepfamily

• Assume that it will take time to adjust to the new roles and expectations of a stepfamily.

• If you're the stepparent, try to build a relationship with your stepchildren slowly over time. Don't move into the role of disciplinarian too quickly. Your best role may be to support the biological parent's parenting and to be a friend or adviser to the kids (to the extent that they let you). Try not to take personally their need or desire not to be close to you. They didn't choose you; their parent did. Even in the best cases, children of divorce can feel a conflict of loyalties.

• If you're the biological parent, try to empathize with your partner about the difficulty of his or her role. Parenting kids you're related to can be hard enough; it's sometimes impossible with kids to whom you're not related.

• Problems with stepkids may not be immediately due to the behavior of the stepparent or the parent. It may be a result of temperamental issues in the child or the child's response to the effects of divorce.

• Don't criticize the parent who isn't in the home to the children or in front of the children. This makes children depressed, anxious, and more likely to have psychological problems.

• If these issues don't appear to get better over time, seek counseling with a professional experienced in stepfamily issues.

> • Read a good self-help book together that deals with divorce and remarriage, such as Constance Ahrons's *The Good Divorce* or E. Mavis Hetherington and John Kelly's *For Better or Worse*. (See References.)

CONCLUSION

IT MAY BE BETTER for you and your children to leave your marriage if you live with domestic violence. Even a high-conflict marriage without physical violence can be harmful to you and your children. If you decide, for now or for the long term, to stay in a high-conflict marriage, you will need a lot of support. If you are able to gain control over your reactions, beliefs, and emotions, you will likely be able to experience more freedom, less anger, and less guilt. This should lead to an improved ability to model healthy behavior in the midst of your partner's outbursts and to provide your children with better parenting from you. The next chapter is written to provide you with the tools and strategies to reduce conflict to determine if you can revitalize your relationship and to show you what to do if you can't.

8

Is Change Possible?

Strategies to revitalize marriage and reduce conflict

I KNOW THAT right now you may be so mad at or alienated from your partner that reaching out is the last thing on your mind. However, the principles of happiness and serenity are based, not only on how you respond to your partner, but on the daily relationship you have with yourself. You may not be able to know whether your marriage can be bettered until you change your behavior consistently for a period of time and observe what happens as a result.

While some marriages end because of overt differences, many wither because couples never develop a way to bring up issues and successfully resolve them. Raising and resolving differences (or at least coming to some kind of accommodation) is one of the most important tools to have in any relationship.

REVITALIZING MARRIAGE

THE FOLLOWING IS a list of recommendations, based on marital research, to help you determine if you can revitalize your marriage. You should read these even if you think that your marriage isn't capable of revitalization, as they contain many important principles for maintaining harmony in the household and in yourself. While change can sometimes take years, do all of the following recommendations for a minimum of six months to see if there is evidence that change is possible in your marriage. Even if your efforts at improving your behavior, thinking, and communication don't cause an improvement in the marriage, it might still get revitalized at a later point, such as when the kids are older or out of the house, or when a crisis resolves. Changes in the beginning will likely be small, but small changes are sometimes evidence that larger changes are possible with more time and effort.

Bearing that in mind, schedule a regular time to talk about your marriage. It should be at a time when you both are free from the stresses of children or work, such as a Sunday evening. Agree to make the meeting brief (less than a half hour) and to work toward keeping it positive. Only raise one issue per meeting and agree to one other meeting in the week if there are other issues. Use the following ground rules:[1]

> Take turns talking and listening without interrupting.
> Don't give advice if it isn't asked for.
> Show interest in what your partner is saying even if you
>   completely disagree with him or her.
> Communicate understanding of your partner's view.
> Take your spouse's side on issues outside of the marriage
>   such as relations with in-laws, employers/employees,
>   friends, etc.
> Express affection.
> Validate your partner's feelings.

Be appreciative of what your partner contributes and what you like or enjoy about him or her. Couples who are unhappy underestimate the frequency of their partner's positive behaviors in the marriage by as much as 50 percent (Gottman 1994, 1999). Be sure to notice and comment frequently and positively on what your partner is doing in any of the following areas:

cleaning
cooking
finances
building and repairing
organizing
parenting (including all of the daily chores that go with
    being a parent, such as making meals, dealing with
    homework, providing nurturance, attending sporting or
    other child events, schlepping them to school, overnights,
    play dates, dentists, doctors, department stores, school
    supply stores, birthday parties, tutors, therapists, learning
    specialists, music lessons, karate . . .)
planning
shopping, etc.

Show interest in your partner's life. If you are aware of an upcoming event that he is either worried or excited about, ask how he is feeling about the event. Showing interest can decrease conflict because it can make your partner know that you're thinking about him. It may also increase positive feelings in the marriage because your spouse may feel more cared about.

Work to appreciate the positive in your partner, even if those traits don't have anything to do with you; these are the qualities that make her unique or interesting, or aspects that you know are important to her. "I notice that you've been doing a lot more art. You're very talented. I really admire that." "It seems like you and your friend, Jane, are getting along again. That must feel good."

If you're mad at your partner, you have likely become less interested in the things that are happening in his life. Thus, when your partner tells you about a conflict with a friend, family member, or coworker, your internal reaction may be to act or feel unconcerned.

However, if he reaches out to you in this way, it may be worthwhile to respond with some show of concern, such as "I'm sorry, that sounds hard," "That must have hurt your feelings," etc. Failing to do so will leave him feeling hurt and rejected and will contribute to a dynamic of distance or hostility.

Avoid criticism when voicing your complaints to your partner. Studies show that 96 percent of the time, conversations end the way they begin (Gottman 1994, 1999). Thus, if you begin your discussion harshly, your partner will likely respond in kind, and the chance for a good resolution has been lost. It's not uncommon for gender differences to emerge during periods of conflict. Women are more likely to raise issues, and men to want to avoid them. Men commonly err on the side of being detached and rational, while women are more likely to criticize or complain about their spouses (Gottman 1994, 1999; Hetherington 2002).

Admit it when you're wrong. It's true that some partners will use this as an opportunity to gloat. So they gloat. The purpose is to find a position that will maximize your serenity and minimize your angst. It's also to model healthy behavior for your children. While there are numerous styles of marriage, the best predictor of a happy and stable marriage is not whether a couple fights, but the ratio of positive to negative experiences.[2] A positive experience can be as simple as an act of affection or a compliment. Other positives are voicing appreciation, doing favors, paying attention to what your partner needs or wants, or expressing concern. You can't control how much your partner extends to you. But you should work to maintain your ratio of positive expressions much higher than your negative expressions.

Pay attention to how you to talk to yourself about your marriage. As Janis Abraham Spring (1997) writes, "Assumptions take on a reality of their own. If you believe your partner is wrong for you and can't change, you're likely to write the relationship off and start looking elsewhere. But if you treat your belief as merely that—a subjective reality that may or may not be true, you can give your partner a chance to prove you wrong. . . . There are no simple answers to the questions, 'Should I change to satisfy my partner?' or 'Should my partner change to satisfy me?' What you're asking of each other could be unreasonable and self-serving, or it could be the catalyst you both need to transcend your old selves, and open the way to a more profound and lasting relationship."

It is likely that you won't want to reach out to your partner in these ways. Once marriages become gridlocked, both wait for the other to change. However, you may not know what your partner is capable of until you have tried these recommendations for a consistent period of time.

MANAGING CONFLICT

IF YOU ARE STAYING because you are concerned about the effects of your children being parented by your partner in a divorce environment, then it's important to make sure that you are a consistent, authoritative, and supportive parent, and that you can adequately protect yourself or your children from harm. The other key ingredient to making this scenario work is getting plenty of outside support so that you are less affected by your partner's behavior. Living with a high-conflict spouse can be very hard on your well-being. You want to be sure that your partner isn't your central source of contact and input. One of the most important keys to making your household a good place for you and your kids is your capacity to manage conflict.

If you have been thinking about changing the dynamic in your marriage but have been avoiding it out of guilt or fear, then the warning voices will get louder as you begin to change. Your mind may marshal a hundred and one perfectly valid reasons why you shouldn't do what you need to. And the smarter and more creative you are, the more convincing and inventive will be your reasons. However, getting control of these warning voices will be liberating in numerous ways. While it may seem impossible given your current feelings, there are ways to begin working on this, starting today. As psychologist Susan Forward writes, "If fear is like a dark river running through you, you can create stepping stones in the midst of that darkness to help yourself across."[3] The following strategies are written to provide you with those stepping stones.

WHEN CONFLICT BEGINS

Begin learning to be one step removed from the reactions and emotions that are currently on automatic pilot (Forward 1987, 1997). Do this by *noticing* what you're feeling in as detached a way as possible. The first step is to notice your reaction without changing it. Some examples of this stage are:

"I'm feeling like I'm a terrible wife and giving in to his demands so I don't have to feel so guilty. *That's interesting.*"

"I'm apologizing to her right now even though I didn't do anything wrong. I'm doing it so that she doesn't have a temper tantrum. *I wonder why.*"

"I'm really defending myself here and blaming him back because I feel so blamed. *I always seem to respond that way.*"

START CHANGING YOUR REACTIONS TO YOUR PARTNER'S BEHAVIOR

The key to changing the dynamic of conflict in the household begins with changing *your* reactions. While you can't change your partner, you can change what happens between the two of you. Begin by considering how you respond to your partner when he or she is difficult:

- I give in.
- I become verbally or physically abusive.
- I get quiet and shut down.
- I take it out on the kids.

- I get the kids to ally with me against my spouse.
- I deny or hide what I'm doing to get out of trouble or stay out of trouble.
- I get confused about who's right or wrong or what is right and wrong.
- I use drugs, alcohol, or food to numb the feelings.
- I get even.

LEARN TO STOP RESPONDING OUT OF EMOTION

Think about what you are willing to do and what you're not. If you're living with someone who is really difficult, it's likely that you're giving in much more frequently than is good for you. It may be useful for you to err on the side of being more self-interested for the next six months until you clearly know whether you are caving in to a demand or agreeing to a demand because it's genuinely unimportant to you.

There are times when it's okay to give in to a partner's demands. One is when you decide it has no negative impact on you or the kids. The other is when you do it as an even trade ("I'll go along with watching the kids alone this weekend so you can go away with your friends, but I want to do the same thing with my friends next month, and I want you to watch the kids for me") or you agree to *part* of the demand ("We can go to your parents' house for dinner, but only if we leave by nine") (Forward 1987, 1997).

In chapter 7, we saw that Antonia felt controlled and dominated by her husband. She needed to gain control over her fear of being abandoned by him before she could be effective in her negotiations. In order to do that, I helped her develop a plan so that she didn't feel so scared. The first step was to have her gain control over her mood and behavior by examining what she was telling herself. I had her keep a log of her thoughts for a week and then had her develop positive counterstatements to her belief system. This is a system proven effective by cognitive therapists such as Aaron Beck and David Burns (Beck 1988; Burns 1997). The goal of the exercise is to:

- become aware of your irrational, self-limiting beliefs
- understand how your emotions are affected by those beliefs
- develop positive counterstatements to the beliefs
- halt the behaviors that are hurtful or self-limiting

In order to apply these techniques to your own life, take a moment to consider what you feel when your partner is critical, blaming, or controlling:

- ashamed
- anxious
- guilt-ridden
- afraid
- enraged
- withdrawn
- depressed
- numb

What do you say to yourself at those times?

"I'm a bad wife/husband/father/mother."
"It's my fault."
"I'll give in this time but next time I won't."
"If I respond, it's only going to get worse."
"He/she is obviously in pain. I should understand."
"I'm going to get him/her."

Write out a positive counterstatement to these beliefs, as I did with Antonia. The goal of this exercise is to have a statement ready to contradict the negative self-statements that you make in response to your partner's treatment. In order to do this, you will need to

FEAR OF ABANDONMENT: ANTONIA

Automatic thought: I'm going to feel too guilty when he gets mad.

Positive counterstatement: I can tolerate guilt. It's not good for me to have my life governed by it.

Automatic thought: He'll retaliate by being distant or withdrawn.

Positive counterstatement: He might. My happiness can't depend on the feedback I get from my partner. It's okay if he's distant and withdrawn. I can learn to tolerate that. That doesn't make me a bad person.

Automatic thought: If I agree to do what he wants, he'll be nicer to me.

Positive counterstatement: Perhaps that's true. However, my life can't be based on whether or not my choices make my partner happy. They have to make me happy, too.

Automatic thought: He's going to be furious. He'll call me every name in the book.

Positive counterstatement: I don't want to be governed by his or other's disapproval. I'm stronger than I give myself credit for. I don't have to stay and listen. I can tell him to knock it off or walk out of the room.

Automatic thought: I need his love. I can't live without it.

Positive counterstatement: If he doesn't love me that would be unfortunate. However, I have others that love and care about me. Besides, how worthwhile is his love if I have to live in a prison for it?

Automatic thought: He's going to leave me, and then where will I be?

> **Positive counterstatement:** He might leave. However, it's harmful to my children and me to live with a constant threat hanging over my head. If he leaves, I'll do whatever it takes to make my life good. It would take hard work, but it would be better than spending the rest of my life ruled by fear and anxiety.

keep a journal for the next two weeks. Make an entry into the journal whenever you have an emotion or become aware of what you're telling yourself. At the end of the two weeks, write out a positive counterstatement to the irrational beliefs, as in the examples on page 195. Then, when you feel bad after an interaction with your partner, determine what you're saying to yourself. Next, repeat the counterstatement to yourself until you start to feel better.[4]

This exercise takes consistent and regular application to be effective. This is because it has to work against your better-learned habit of buying into another's criticism or mistreatment of you. It requires a commitment to note and address self-critical comments when they enter your head. While this may seem like it's going to take a lot of energy and commitment, that's only because all of your energy and commitment are currently going to being hard on yourself, believing others when they are hard on you, or angrily disproving them in your mind. This exercise may be confusing at first because you may believe most of the mean things that you tell yourself, even though some part of you recognizes them as irrational.

Forward (1987) recommends moving away from a deferential position in marriage, where you request permission with statements and questions such as

"Is this okay?"
"Do you agree?"
"Do you like it?"
"Would you mind if . . . ?"

Date• Situation• Emotion• Behavior• Automatic thought• Positive self-statement

Date: Friday.
Situation: Husband yelled at me for twenty minutes because I locked keys in car.
Emotion: Sadness, despair, resentment.
Behavior: Withdrew, isolated.
Automatic thought: I'm a bad wife/person.
Positive self-statement: I'm a good person whether my partner is mad at me or not. Anybody can lock their keys in the car.
New behavior: Be assertive when he is being critical. Either get him to stop or walk away from the situation.

Date: Last weekend.
Situation: Wife shamed me in front of our friends at dinner.
Emotion: Anger/rage.
Automatic thought: I'm going to get her.
Positive self-statement: Revenge keeps me mired in the cycle of unhappiness. It's also a destructive model for my children. I choose to respond in a way that makes me feel good about myself.
New behavior: Channel my anger in a healthy way, either by assertively telling her that she can't talk to me like that, through stress-reducing activities, or both.

to more assertive statements such as

"This is what I believe."
"This is what I think."

WANT LIST: ANTONIA

I want more say over decisions regarding money and where
we take vacations.

I want to go back to school.

I want more help with the kids when you get home in the
evening.

I want you to state your complaints about me as complaints
and not criticisms.

I want us to go out once a week.

I want more say over where we go and what we do when we
go out.

I want more affection before sex.

"This is what I will do."

"This is what I will not do."

"This is what I want."

It may also be useful to develop a Want List to help orient yourself to what will make you happier in life and marriage. For example, Antonia and I developed the above Want List for her.

TIME-OUTS

During a calm moment, tell your partner that you want to find a way to have more harmony in the household. Say something like, "I want to find a way to manage our conflicts so that they don't get out of control. How about whenever we have a fight, either of us can call a time-out if it's starting to get too uncomfortable? A time-out means one or both of us leave the room and we avoid contact until we both agree to reconnect. I recommend that whoever calls the time-out agrees to approach the other within a specified period of time, no longer than twenty-four hours." The purpose of the time-out is for both partners to cool down and allow each to get into a more rational state of mind.[5]

As a general rule, you should call a time-out when your interaction starts to feel uncomfortable and unproductive. If your partner doesn't yield to a time-out, say clearly and strongly, "Stop yelling!" or "Knock it off!" Warn her once that you are going to walk out if she can't speak calmly. If it persists, leave the room, or the house if need be. Don't allow yourself to be pulled into a useless argument.

In general, the goal is to avoid an escalating fight. When you defend yourself, you give your partner power over how you react. When you react without justifying your behavior, you reclaim your power over the interaction.

DEALING WITH THREATS AND CRITICISM

Sometimes the best response to a threat is no response. Responding to threatening, critical, or hurtful behavior in a reactive way almost always escalates a situation. In addition, it increases the likelihood that the fight will become more about your reaction than your partner's poor behavior. However, if you, for whatever reason, feel that you have to respond to threats, say something like "I hope you don't" or "Maybe you'll feel differently later." Another strategy is to comment on the behavior: "I know you're really upset about this." "You're angry, I understand that. I still have to do what I think is best." "Threatening me won't help." The main thing is to respond in a way that allows you to avoid getting pulled into the drama because outside the drama is where you can think the most clearly and strategize the most effectively.

Some of the most common threats in marriage are to divorce, take the kids, or leave the other partner penniless. Other common threats are to have an affair, shame the partner to his or her family or friends, tell everyone of some secret, or commit suicide or other self-harm. Don't provoke your partner if he or she's threatening you by saying statements like "Good! I'll see you in court!" "You couldn't have an affair because nobody else would want you!" "If you're gonna kill yourself, go ahead." Threats are made when people feel the most desperate and insecure. They are also made by partners who believe that threats work, based on prior experience in the marriage (Walker 1984; Weitzman 2000). Humiliating your partner in response to his or her attempts to control or humiliate you increases the likelihood of the situation spiraling out of control. This type of fight is particularly troubling to children (Cummings and Cummings 1988).

It is possible that when your partner gets angry or critical of you, his or her intention is to solve a problem, not to hurt you (Burns 1999). In other words, it may be a request for you to change that has some merit. Thus, conflict can often be defused by going on a fact-finding mission to get to the bottom of the attack. A key technique is the use of empathy. Here is an example.

Wife: "The thing I can't stand about you is how lazy you are."

Husband: "What is it about me that you think is lazy?" (Fact-finding rather than defending or attacking. Communicates interest in her complaint.)

"You don't do anything around the house."

"I know I don't do as much as you want and that can be hard on you. What is it that you want me to do more of?" (Empathy and more interest in her complaint.)

"Everything."

"Can you tell me more specifically? I want to get it right." (Expressing interest without buying into the attacks.)

"Why should I have to? You live here too! I'm tired of being your mother. I already have two kids, I don't need another one."

"Well, you're right, you shouldn't have to. I just think I can address your complaint better if I know what would be the most meaningful to you."

"Help more with the kids."

"Okay, I can do that. Let's sit down tonight and draw up a list of five to ten things that would be helpful."

In this situation, his wife had a legitimate complaint that her husband wasn't helping her enough. However, she had been putting her complaints in the form of an attack because she felt too guilt-ridden and undeserving to ask for help directly. Once her husband began using this technique, he could address her complaints without counterblaming or attacking her. The more that her husband didn't get defensive, the more she was able to calm down and be specific in her requests. Research shows that not getting defensive while your partner voices a complaint or criticism greatly increases the probability of a successful outcome (Gottman 1994), especially if you are listening and reflecting in a way that makes it clear that you want to address your partner's concerns.

A key to good empathizing is to avoid getting into who's "right or wrong" during arguments. The goal isn't to win, it's to live your life in a way that isn't controlled or dominated by your partner's behavior. The issue is who you want to be in your marriage. Psychiatrist David Burns writes in *Feeling Good*, "If the person is very hot under the collar, he or she may be hurling labels at you, perhaps even obscenities. Nevertheless, ask for more information. What do those words mean? Why does the person call you a "no good shit"? How did you offend this individual? What did you do? When did you do it? How often have you done it? What else does the person dislike about you?" Burns's example shows a way to be more detached and less caught up in the drama of the fight. Your role becomes more of an investigator than someone who has to prove his innocence.

In some cases, it's useful to agree with the criticism or accusation. If your partner accuses you of being selfish, you can respond by saying, "Sometimes I am selfish. That's true." Don't go into moral outrage and bring out a hundred and one reasons why you're a saint. In almost all of our partner's complaints, however poorly presented, there is some kernel of truth (Hendrix 1988). Admitting that you can be selfish is not the same as saying, "Yes, I am a selfish jerk. You've been right all along." It's saying to yourself, "Yes, I am selfish sometimes. I'm still a good person." Acknowledging this kernel can defuse a volatile situation because it increases the likelihood that your partner will feel validated by your taking his or her complaints seriously. It's possible that your spouse has no idea how hurt, shut down, or discouraged you feel. This may be true for a variety of reasons. One is that you haven't clearly communicated the degree of your upset because you feel afraid to hurt her feelings, because you have been too intimidated, or because you feel too undeserving to complain.

Another way to reduce conflict is to *ask for your partner's help* (Forward 1997). Asking for help immediately puts the conflict into a context where you're telling your partner he is needed. It reduces your partner's fears that you're raising the issues as a way to point out his inadequacy or criticize him. This may be especially useful with husbands because men are more likely to get defensive when they're being told something rather than being asked to help (Tannen 1990). This isn't to say that you act in a submissive manner. Rather, you begin the interaction with the assumption of cooperation.

BE ASSERTIVE IN YOUR NEGOTIATING

Once you have reduced the conflict and moved the conversation to a calmer place, assert your requests. One technique is to stick with your position, and simply *repeat* it. Assertiveness trainers refer to this as the *broken-record technique*. Don't allow yourself to be scared away from what you want; however, be willing to compromise.

ELEVEN WAYS TO WORK ON YOURSELF

IT'S TEMPTING to give up on marriage because it's just too much damned work. I hear a lot of people say, "Look, it's hard enough making a living and getting my kids raised; I just don't have the energy to do all of this self-analysis and behavior change." You get to decide; you don't have to change if you don't want to. But there are very real benefits to you and your children if you do. Unfortunately, there aren't that many shortcuts in developing as a person. Change is usually slow and time-consuming, but frankly, what isn't in life that's worth pursuing? Getting and staying in shape, learning to play a musical instrument, maintaining a spiritual life, raising children, getting an education? Sure, it's a lot of work, but look at the gains. The following recommendations are made to help you work on your goals, regardless of the state of your relationship.

1. **Be accountable to yourself.** Cultivate the awareness that you can change your life. Even though the past can feel as though it predicts the future, it doesn't have to. Give yourself the gift of discovering that daily discipline toward your goals pays off in important life changes.

2. **Overcome the hidden rewards of not changing.** To grow, you may have to surrender a dynamic with your partner that gives you more control, more dominance, more dependency, or more financial benefits. Presently, your problems may get you more attention or emotional comfort in the marriage than does your growth or success. Evaluate to what extent this is true and make a commitment to yourself to do without it.

3. **Make a commitment to follow through.** Be a good friend to yourself by committing to do what you say you'll do to change. This means keeping yourself to a regular schedule and not getting distracted, especially by others' needs. Children are a great excuse to avoid changing your life. "I don't have time because I'm so busy with the kids." "They come first." "They won't like it." Cultivate an abundance mentality where there is enough for everyone, and you're not the last in line.

4. **Take risks.** Assume that whatever behavior you're changing is going to feel foreign, forbidden, and scary as hell. As the author Susan Jeffers (1987) says, "Feel the fear and do it anyway." Fear is almost always based on an irrational worry from childhood. Develop a dialogue with your fears so that you're in charge of them rather than their being in charge of you. Read Lewis Engel and Tom Fer-

guson's *Hidden Guilt,* Irwin Gootnick's *Why You Behave in Ways You Hate: And What You Can Do About It.* David Burns's *Feeling Good,* or Edmund Bourne's *The Anxiety and Phobia Workbook* for more techniques on combating irrational fears. (See References).

5. **Take pride in each small step of growth or change.** If you told your husband no for the first time in five years, don't follow it up with self-shaming remarks such as "Well, I should have done it sooner" or "So, big deal. I finally told him no." Be a good parent to yourself. If you did something new, take the time to pat yourself on the back. Brag to a friend or anyone else who would take pleasure in your accomplishments. That's how self-esteem is built and solidified.

6. **Expect setbacks.** Change never occurs in a straight line upward. It's always a sawtooth curve. Expect that some weeks will be two steps forward, one step back, while other weeks it will be no steps forward and four steps back.

7. **Don't push yourself to change too quickly.** Change is rarely achieved overnight, and important changes can sometimes take years to accomplish. Don't get impatient with yourself. Change is like learning to play an instrument. You don't sit down to the piano for the first time and start playing a Bach fugue. First you have to find middle C, and then build upward from there.

8. **Visualize the changes as a way to increase your confidence with succeeding.** Sports psychologists have shown that visualizing success can increase the chances of succeeding (Spino 1979). The goal of this is to replace the critical and pessimistic movie that's currently playing with a positive image of who you'd like to be and what you'll be doing.

9. **Learn how to soothe yourself and relax.** Learn how to soothe yourself so that your anxiety is not such a dominant feature of your emotional landscape by using self-talk, affirmations, and relaxation techniques. Research shows that the practice of deep relaxation on a daily basis for twenty to thirty minutes can make you feel more relaxed for the rest of the day (Benson 1985; LeShan 1974). Yoga,

exercise, and meditation have all been found to be effective tools to develop a more relaxed state of mind.

10. **Move past workaholism.** Our culture prizes work above everything. At the same time, we have moved from a parent-centered household to a child-centered household. This puts parents in the dilemma of working longer hours than they ever have and feeling more guilty about the effects of this on their children (Eh-rensaft 1997). As a result, parents feel the need to be on all of the time and are more burned-out than ever.

11. **Manage your time.** Time management can be achieved by prioritizing, delegating responsibility, allowing extra time, letting go of perfectionism, overcoming procrastination, and saying *no* to non-critical demands (Bourne 2000). Reinvest that time in self-care and nurturance.

9

Different Kinds of Marriage

Intimates, friends, or roommates?

"Fred and I don't have a very intimate marriage. We do things together as a family, but other than that, it's more like a friendship than a real relationship. I can't say it's what I hoped for, but I've made peace with it, and that's been better for me and the kids."
—EVELYN, AGE THIRTY-TWO

"Millie and I have a pretty good marriage these days. It's a surprise to me because there were plenty of times when we almost split up."
—STEVE, AGE FORTY-FOUR

"Jack is impossible to live with most of the time but I've decided to stay together because I think it's better for the kids than if we break up."
—ANNALEE, AGE TWENTY-SIX

IF YOU'RE MARRIED long enough, your feelings about your marriage may change from year to year, or even from day to day. While your relationship may change in the future, it's important to know where you are *right now*. My clinical experience is that marriages are characterized by one of the five following types:

1. *Capable of revitalization*
2. *Coparent friends*
3. *Roommates*
4. *Constant battlers*
5. *Covert fighters*

This chapter is written to help you decide which category you fit into and to make a plan for going forward.

TWO KINDS OF ACCEPTANCE

ACCEPTANCE OF YOUR PARTNER and acceptance of yourself are the two most important ingredients to a peaceful household. There are two types of acceptance in marriage. The first is when we accept our mates while we strive for more intimacy, involvement, and depth. In this scenario we work to understand our spouses at the same time that we do everything we can to have our needs addressed in the marriage. This means learning how to communicate more effectively, examining how our behavior affects the marriage, and trying to rekindle what was once positive in the marriage. It is based on the assumption that our goals for the marriage are reasonable and realistic, based on who we are and whom we have chosen as partners. In this case, there is reason to believe that the marriage is capable of revitalization.

In the second scenario, you accept your partner while also accepting that he or she can't give you what you need and want. This presumes that you've tried everything to have more of what you want *and* have solid reason to believe that it isn't going to happen. This doesn't mean that you've told your best friends what a jerk he is and they all agree that you should dump the loser. This also doesn't mean that you've dipped a few toes in the water of trying to change your behavior and concluded that it's too cold to go in. It means that you have examined your communication style, that you are fully aware of your own liabilities and limitations, and that you have a reasonably empathic view of who he or she is based on a solid understanding of his or her childhood or other important formative experiences. Most of all, it means that you have given the marriage time to grow, change, and develop.

CAPABLE OF REVITALIZATION

MY CLINICAL EXPERIENCE is that most, though not all, marriages are capable of some renewed vitality and connection. Feeling hopeless is not, in and of itself, a sign that you're in the wrong marriage or that you're doomed to a life without intimacy. Feeling stuck in marriage is part of everyone's bargain, if we're married long enough. Often this can be a place of growth because you're forced to reveal more of who you are to yourself and your partner—to say this is where I'm vulnerable, this is what turns me on, this is where I feel alienated.

In the marriage that is *capable of revitalization,* your feelings of hopelessness may stem from a crisis or state of gridlock; however, there are significant strengths in your relationship, and with therapy, working on your issues, or the passage of time, you will be able to work it out. You may once have had loving or romantic feelings toward your partner, but haven't found a way back to what was good between you. This could result from a job loss or job change, financial threat, the loss of an important loved one, difficulty separating from parents, the arrival of children, or an affair, to name a few.

> Wendy: My marriage was pretty good before kids but got bad after we had our girls. I would say I thought about divorce all of the time during the first eight years of being a mother. It wasn't until I came close to acting on a flirtation at work that I realized something had to change quick, and I made Brandon go to couple's therapy with me. It was rough at first because we both had built up a lot of resentment for each other over the years. But I was surprised to find that we've been able to recover a lot of what we once had. I'm remembering why I married him.

Sometimes good marriages become alienated, not as a result of a particular crisis or situation, but because the personality differences between the partners cause each to adopt positions which make intimacy difficult. This creates a negative feedback loop that gets more rigid over time. These differences can be lessened when there is a shift in the dynamic in the couple.

> Samuel: Tina's a superorganized person, which I found really attractive in the beginning. After five years of marriage, though, I started feeling like she was the most controlling person in the world, and I really couldn't stand being around her. I'm kind of messy, and I felt like, "It's my home too and I can be a slob if I want to." I just kind of gave up on caring what she thought, and she seemed to feel the same way about me. The more she complained about me, the lazier I got. I don't know why, but about a year ago she started trying really hard to work on the marriage. She started acting really sweet to me, and being more relaxed, and that made me want to start trying too. So after all of this time, it seems like we're getting close again.

In order to revitalize your marriage, both of you may have to be willing to work on it, though sometimes a lot can be done with only one motivated partner, as the above example shows. Beware of the game played by so many couples, called "You change first and then I'll change," or its petulant cousin, "I've already changed enough, so now it's your turn." It may be that changing yourself will be enough to shift out of a difficult dynamic between you. You may also have to force your partner into individual or couple's therapy, get into your own individual therapy, get gentler, get tougher, or get more detached in order to make the changes in yourself that could revitalize your marriage. As sociologist Linda Waite's research shows, many individuals become more satisfied with marriage over time because the couple works hard to make it better, because they outlast their problems, or because one or both of the partners is able to successfully pursue happiness despite significant marital difficulties (Waite, 2002).

MARRIAGES THAT AREN'T CAPABLE OF REVITALIZATION

NOT ALL MARRIAGES are capable of being deeply satisfying. You may have spent a lot of time trying to revitalize your marriage and now have to grieve that your marriage will never be what you hoped for. In this case, you may need to accept that your marriage will be more like a friendship, or even like being roommates. Either way, acceptance of your partner (and yourself) is the key. As awful as people can behave in marriage, the vast majority would try to make their partners happy if they were capable of it, and if it didn't put them at psychological risk. This is illustrated by the case of Bob and Mary.

> Bob: I know Mary would like it if I could show her more of my feelings. But I've never been a really emotional person and I don't think I ever will be. The idea of getting all in touch with my feelings and showing them isn't something I have any interest in doing. I don't think that's something that's going to change.

Mary is furious at Bob for not being more demonstrative. She berates him in front of the children, which causes him to retreat even further. If Mary were with a partner who was more affectionate, and more comfortable talking about his feelings, she might feel less lonely in her marriage and respond in a different manner. Unfortunately, she chose someone who is very closed down. She could decide that it's too painful to stay with him and divorce him. If she's going to stay married, however, she'll have to change her view of Bob and herself in order to gain happiness. She will need to accept that Bob will likely never be the way she wants him to be. And if he'll change, it will come only if she stops getting mad at him all of the time.

Ideally, Bob would be healthy enough to reassure Mary that it isn't her fault that he's not more responsive. That would go a long way toward helping Mary feel cared about and get her to stop blaming herself and him. Mary would also be helped by thinking of Bob's behavior as an *inability* rather than an *unwillingness* to show her more of his feelings. Perceiving it as unwillingness makes her feel victimized by his behavior. It also makes her more likely to continue to get rejected and disappointed, because she's operating from the assumption that if she only tries hard enough, he'll cough up the goods.

WHEN PEOPLE DON'T WANT TO CHANGE

MOST PEOPLE ARE CAPABLE of some change *if* they are willing to do the work to make it happen. However, without that work, there may be very real limitations to how intimate, verbal, carefree, ambitious, or sexual a partner can be. Change requires consistently applied effort to a goal that is often not immediately attainable. For example, if a man is afraid of closeness because he was humiliated during his childhood, he may be unwilling to revisit those memories in order to understand the walls he erected to protect himself from that pain. He might not know that his defenses are guarding him around the clock, attacking, questioning, interrogating, and repelling all would-be friends and foes alike. He might not see that those defenses have outlived the useful purpose they once served of protecting him from a terrible threat.

Long-term change almost always occurs through risk of rejection, guilt, or shame, and the integration of the information gained from that risk. Through risk and experimentation with new behavior, he could learn that these defenses have outlived their usefulness and could be replaced by vulnerability and accessibility. *If* he were willing. It's just that not everyone is. That may be something you have to grieve for and accept about your partner. If you find that you do all of the recommendations in this book for a period of time, and your marriage still doesn't improve, then your marriage likely falls into one of the next four categories.

THE COPARENT FRIENDS AND ROOMMATES HOUSEHOLDS

IN THE COPARENT FRIENDS household, there is a lot that you like or even love about your partner; however, it isn't enough to outweigh your strong feelings of loneliness, or lack of attraction to him or her. In this scenario, you parent reasonably well together and are generally compatible in the overall priorities and management of the house.

> Jill: Mark is a good guy. I can't imagine a better dad for the girls. It's just that I'm not really in love with him and I probably never was. I doubt he even knows I feel that way other than the fact that I never want to have sex. He's just off in his own world all of the time and I tend to feel alone a lot in the marriage.

With *coparent friends*, there are activities that you enjoy together as a family; however, your time with each other isn't meaningful in a way that you would strongly prefer. You may already have tried couple's or individual therapy and been unsuccessful at revitalizing your marriage. Some marriages remain in this state because one or both members are unable to take the kind of risks necessary to deepen the marriage.

In the *roommates* household, there is a large amount of distance in the marriage, but you are generally able to protect your children from your differences or areas of dissatisfaction. This means that you don't behave in a martyred, victimized, or hostile fashion, as in the high-conflict relationships of the constant battlers and covert fighters. Your distance may stem from a long-term problem in the marriage that has never been successfully addressed or resolved. You may have had intimacy at one point in your marriage and outgrew your partner, or discovered that your partner had obstacles to intimacy of which you were unaware, such as psychiatric or addiction problems. There may also have been betrayals or conflicts that affect your or your partner's willingness to remain interested in working on your relationship.

All of these dissatisfactions could exist in a marriage that is *capable of revitalization* or a *coparent friends* marriage, but in the *roommates* household, there are more serious reasons for your pessimism. While you participate in some of the children's activities together, your inability to enjoy each other's company or successfully resolve problems makes time together unworkable. As a result, one or both of you likely works late or spends time away from the marriage with hobbies or friends.

> Benjamin: Shoshanna and I have really separate lives. We got married for all of the wrong reasons. I stay married to her because I want to be with my kids all of the time, and if we got divorced I wouldn't be able to. Plus, divorce would be a disaster, financially, for both of us.

In a *roommates* marriage, it's likely that you wouldn't share vacations or do elaborate gift-giving during birthdays or anniversaries. Because of your separateness from each other, it's unlikely that either of you would be greatly aware of or interested in the other's conflicts or aspirations. Here, as with *coparent friends*, the obstacle to becoming more intimate may exist because one of you prefers the distance, or is emotionally incapable of a more intimate connection. You may never have been very interested in your partner, and married for reasons that were less central to intimacy, such as a desire for financial security, a need to leave home, a concern that you were getting too old to have children, or pressure from your parents or friends. While many marry for these reasons and still find their way to a satisfying marriage, many don't.

In some households that are *coparent friends* or *roommates*, a parent is gay or lesbian, and either realized it later in the marriage, or married during a time or place where gay parenting was more forbidden. A partner may have married before there were the reproductive options that exist today for gay couples such as ovum donation, sperm donation, and surrogacy, and a heterosexual marriage was the only avenue to be a parent or to achieve societal acceptance.

With both *coparent* friends and *roommates*, it's possible that you or your spouse will want to separate once the kids are in college. Nevertheless, you are able to protect your children from the obvious negative effects of your differences, even though the dissatisfaction you feel about your marriage is moderate to serious. Your children likely don't know the degree of your unhappiness, nor would your friends if you haven't told them.

CONSTANT BATTLERS AND COVERT FIGHTERS

IT IS NOT ALWAYS BETTER for children for their parents to stay married (Amato, Loomis, and Booth 1995; Jekielek 1998). In the marriages of the *constant battlers* and *covert fighters,* your relationship is hard not only on you; it's hard on your children because your conflict is so intense, chronic, overt, and unresolved. It may be in the best interest of you and/or your kids for you to leave your marriage if there is no other way to protect them, physically or psychologically. While the structure of your marriage may be more like roommates in terms of shared time or activities, you are unable to isolate your children from the problems in your marriage.

In the *constant battlers* marriage, there is overt hostility constantly expressed by both of you, in front of the children. There may have been a number of serious transgressions over the course of the marriage, such as ongoing physical violence toward each other or the kids, ongoing public affairs, flagrant misuse of family funds, or serious violations of confidences.

> Madeline: I may have to leave Sheldon. He's always screaming at me or the kids and I can't take it. I'm no angel either—I scream right back; our fights are really brutal, and I know the

kids are really upset by how much we fight. The other day my eldest teen asked me why we don't break up. It was really upsetting.

The *constant battlers* marriage can be confusing for some couples because the terrible times may be followed by passionate periods of sex or making up.

In the second form of high conflict, *covert fighters,* you and your partner express unhappiness about the marriage *through* your children, though in a more covert fashion. Your kids are frequently put in the middle of your conflicts even though those conflicts aren't loud or chaotic. You often use your child to communicate to your partner. Both you and your spouse may attempt to get needs met through the children that you are unable to get through each other, such as ongoing validation for your feeling hurt or angry at the other partner, companionship, or affection in a way that is harmful to them. In your household, your children feel forced or obligated to choose sides.

In the high-conflict marriages of both the *constant battlers* and the *covert fighters,* you may be staying because of financial worries, religious reasons, threat of physical harm, or a fear of how divorce would affect you or the kids. In both scenarios, your goal, if you stay, is to reduce the conflict so that your children are not emotionally or physically harmed. Your and your children's safety has to be the first priority.

OTHER OPTIONS GOING FORWARD

CONFLICT IN MARRIAGE exists on a continuum. In some cases, if the issues are seriously addressed by one or both of you, you may be able to revitalize your marriage or make your marriage into *co-parent friends* or *roommates.* If you are unable to shift your marriage in a more positive direction, you may need to reduce the amount of time that you spend with your partner. This can be done either through an *in-house separation* or, if that is unsuccessful, a *therapeutic separation*.

IN-HOUSE SEPARATION

Some couples are able to discuss openly how they are going to structure their marriage so that they can stay together, despite obvious incompatibility or lack of satisfaction. In this scenario, you and your partner agree that you are temporarily or permanently incompatible, and that you are giving up on a marriage founded on intimacy. You may also decide that you're still open to intimacy but, for whatever reason, are unable to work successfully on your differences for the time being. An in-house separation means that while you may still occasionally do activities as a family, your free time will likely be spent away from your partner. If you aren't able to spend time together as a family, then you agree to live in the same house and not spend much time together. If you have a hard time being in the same room without fighting, you may find it useful to split the time spent with the children on the weekend or in the evenings.

This scenario means detaching yourself from expectations of intimacy from your partner and expectations that you should provide it in return. Some couples have explicit agreements that allow outside relationships. While there are occasionally couples who can successfully manage this terrain, most are unsuccessful. This is because once it's clear that either person is involved outside of the marriage, feelings of jealousy and betrayal typically surface. In addition, there is a likelihood that an outside relationship will become serious, triggering a divorce. Thus, if you and your partner are going to have outside relationships and want to discuss this with each other, you should be very clear about your terms. You should also be clear that your marriage may not survive it.

An in-house separation has many of the properties of a divorce with shared custody. Therefore, if you and your partner are able, sit down together and go over all of the potential areas of conflict and misunderstanding. This may also mean talking about a long-term financial plan if you're considering divorce once the kids leave home. You may need a neutral third party to help you with these interactions.

Typically, one person is more motivated to stay in the marriage or continue working on it (Ahrons 2002). If you're the one who no longer wants to work on the marriage, it may be useful to be direct with your spouse. Tell him or her that you have tried hard to work it out, you don't want a divorce, but it clearly no longer makes sense to keep on trying to meet each other's needs for change or intimacy; it only seems to make you both more unhappy.

> Evan: Ursula and I decided recently that while we don't want to divorce, we want to stop pretending that we're compatible. So our plan is to stay together until our son is out of the house, and then we'll probably split up. It feels better this way because we can both stop acting like we're working on the marriage when it doesn't seem like either of us is working on it.

In the case where your partner will become abusive or controlling, or where he or she may push for divorce, it may be better to not discuss your intentions for an in-house separation. In this case, you should direct your energies to containing his or her problematic behavior and to work on being detached from the ways that your partner is difficult for you. In-house separations aren't recommended for a marriage that is still capable of revitalization, where your energies should be going toward increasing intimacy. If you are unable to be successful with an in-house separation, you may have to consider a therapeutic separation.

THERAPEUTIC SEPARATION

Some couples have to live separately for a time. One reason to suggest a separation is to make a clear statement about your need for change from a partner who has thus far ignored your heartfelt, sincere, and reasonable efforts to be different. An example might be an out-of-control alcoholic or addict who refuses to get into recovery; a depressed, narcissistic, or abusive spouse who refuses to enter individual or couple's work; or someone with a mental illness who refuses to go on medication or stay on it. You suggest a separation if you believe that you're headed there anyway if something doesn't change in your marriage, or because you need the time to gain clarity over your own behavior, or the behavior of your spouse.

> Lynette: Victor and I have fought for years, and we finally decided to try a separation. It was obvious how bad our fighting was for the kids. I have no idea whether a separation is going to help or not, but living together didn't seem to be good for us or the kids.

A therapeutic separation means you agree that one of you will move out for a period of two to six months. The goal is to determine if time apart allows one or both of you to either cool down, change, or appreciate what you have. During that time you should both engage in individual and couple's therapy to maximize whatever insight or awareness that surfaces. Sometimes separating can give you enough space to reclaim some important part of yourself that was buried in the marriage, such as your self-esteem, your identity, or your joy for living without putting everyone else's needs before yours. Once that part is reclaimed, you may feel better able to reenter marriage on a stronger footing. You or your partner may also get insight into ways that you have been contributing to the problems in your relationship that weren't as clear because you were spending so much energy fending off each other's unhappiness, accusations, or guilt trips.

In addition, a separation may allow you both to see how much each of you positively contributes to the marriage. A husband might appreciate the difficulty of being a parent once his wife is removed from planning and organizing all of his or the children's activities. Similarly, a wife may more greatly value her husband's financial or organizational contributions if he isn't around to help her.

Sometimes the act of *planning* to separate can cause an improvement in the marriage.

Timothy: I debated for years whether to stay with Lilly or not. We did everything to try to keep it together for the kids' sake: self-help, couple's therapy, workshops. Nothing helped. Finally I said, "I can't take this anymore," and I signed a lease on an apartment and decided to move out, at least for a while. Surprisingly, that shifted something between us, and it's been better since without me ever moving out. I don't know whether Lilly changed or I changed, but something about walking up to that abyss and deciding to jump in made things better between us.

On the other hand, there is the possibility that one of you will like the separation enough to want to move it forward to divorce. If you're the one initiating the separation, it should be because you have reason to believe that it will be a good wake-up call to your partner, because you think you're headed for divorce and it's a final effort, or because you know that you can't continue living with your partner.

Suggesting a therapeutic separation can be a useful ultimatum. However, an ultimatum should be used only after you've reasonably exhausted all avenues of change, and if you are willing to follow through.

Travis: Kimberly was a serious drinker and a mean drunk. After putting up with it for so many years, I finally felt like, enough is enough. I told her, "I can't continue to live under the same roof with you and have you talk to me or the kids in the way that you do. You get to choose if you're going to drink, but I get to choose if I want to live with you. If you don't get into recovery then I want a separation." Once she knew I meant business she actually got into recovery, and she's been going ever since.

Obviously, it doesn't always work out that way. That's why you don't suggest a separation until you're willing and able to act on it.

TELLING THE KIDS ABOUT A THERAPEUTIC SEPARATION

In general, you should be direct about an imminent plan to separate. "Your dad and I haven't been getting along very well for a while. We're going to try living separately for the next few months and continue to work on the marriage. We'll both make an effort to continue seeing you as much as before. This has nothing to do with anything either of you has done. It has to do with how we get along." Allow and encourage their questions and reactions. Your children may react strongly to your announcing or enacting a separation, depending on their age and their temperament.

IF YOU PLAN TO SEPARATE OR DIVORCE AFTER YOUR CHILDREN ARE GROWN

If you think that you are heading for a divorce or separation once your kids are grown, it's important to begin financial planning for you and for them. If you and your spouse agree that you will eventually separate, then you should work together to have a long-range plan that takes both of your needs into account. Ideally, you would meet with a tax attorney or financial planner in order to develop long-term goals. The more common scenario is that you will have to make a plan without your partner's knowledge or consent.

If your spouse has the ability to hide assets or in some other way use his or her wealth or power against you, you will need long-term help to best prevent this from occurring. While you have to enjoy your life while you're married, you may also want to avoid making expensive purchases that will depreciate over time, such as cars, jewelry, clothing, etc. If it's likely that you're going to leave once the kids are grown, you have to see all of your decisions through that lens.

My clinical experience is that when parents divorce, it can be confusing for children of any age. A consistent finding is that parental divorce greatly increases the likelihood of offspring divorce (Amato and Booth 1997; Hetherington 2002; Wallerstein, Lewis, and Blakeslee 2000). While most of the research has been done on the effects of divorce while children are under the age of eighteen, one large study found that if the children are teens or out of the house when a divorce occurs, the chance of their divorcing as adults is higher than if their parents divorce before the children are twelve (Amato and Booth 1997).

You may be able to help your children by taking full responsibility for their confusion if you split up after they are grown. Let them know that you wanted to insulate them from the problems in your marriage (in the case where those problems weren't obvious) and for that reason didn't let them know that you had been considering divorce for a long time. This kind of discussion may make them feel guilty that you stayed unhappily married for their sake. They may feel responsible for your making a decision in their interest that affected your ability to be fulfilled in other parts of your life. You should make it absolutely clear that staying was a decision you did for yourself as well. "I wanted to be able to have every day that I could with you. If we had divorced when you were young, it would have been hard on you and me. We all make compromises in life and this was one that I was happy to make."

If you have a high-conflict marriage where your children are often loudly exposed to the bitter unhappiness in your life, and positive interchanges are rare or nonexistent, this argument will be less persuasive to older kids. They may argue (and maybe not incorrectly) that both you and they might have been better served by a divorce. If you waited until they were out of the house before you divorced, they will likely experience a range of emotions: anger that you didn't do it sooner and spare them, relief that you're finally taking care of yourself, sadness that their childhood home or family is being changed. It's rarely simple.

It's not uncommon for children who are old enough to learn who's leaving whom to be angry or resentful of the parent who wants the divorce, especially in a low-conflict situation where your unhappiness was less obvious. An adult child who grew up with parents who seemed compatible, but then split up, may question his powers of perception—he may wonder why he couldn't see it while it was happening. It may make him feel anxious that a future marital partner would want a divorce and he wouldn't see it coming. In this situation, the child could experience your desire for a divorce or separation as selfish.

Whether you're ending a low- or a high-conflict marriage, you should strive to be empathic to your children's reactions if they express anger, hurt, or sadness about your decision. They have a right to their reactions in the same way that you have a right to make decisions about your marriage. Don't defend yourself or tell them that you did it for them, so they should be grateful. If they say you should have done it sooner, tell them that maybe you should have; you were trying to make the best decision you could for the family and yourself. Tell them you understand that they will have a range of reactions to your decision and you're open to hearing all of their feelings. Let them know that you understand that it may take a long time for them to heal, and you're committed to doing whatever it takes to help them on that path.

If your children are mad at you, make sure you get a lot of support. My experience working with families is that there is nothing so potentially volatile as when an adult child starts to review the mistakes or choices of a parent to that parent (Coleman 2000). If you sacrificed a significant portion of your life to spare your children the difficulties of divorce, and they get mad at you for doing it once they're grown, or they get mad at you for not doing it sooner, you will have to work very hard not to get defensive. A common reaction I have witnessed in my office from parents is, "What?! Do you have any idea how much I gave up for you? Do you think it was easy living with your father/mother? Do you know how lonely I was all of those years and how many times I wanted to throw up my hands and say, 'I'm outta here, but didn't, just to save you kids from the heartache of a divorce? And now you tell me I'm selfish to finally want my own life or that I should have done it sooner?" That would be a completely understandable reaction for you to have. It's just not for their ears.

A MIND-SET FOR GOING FORWARD

IF YOU AREN'T ABLE to revitalize your marriage and you decide to stay married for the sake of your children for the long or short term, you will need a new belief system to orient you to this new way of being together. The following statements are written to help you with this process.

- I will stop looking to my partner as a source of intimacy for now, and maybe forevermore.
- I will grieve for the loss of the marriage I thought I'd have, and stop bemoaning what I'm not getting from my partner.
- I will work hard to develop my life because that will be the best remedy for resisting my partner's negative pull on me, or my destructive need for him or her.
- I will work to examine my counterproductive beliefs about marriage as being central to my happiness.

- I will work to keep the tone of my household calm and in control because that is what's best for my children and me. While I don't have control over my partner's behavior, I have control over my own.
- I may have to accept that sex with my partner will be rare, nonexistent, or less satisfying than I would like.
- I will give up my addiction to being right.
- I will stop hoping that my partner will change and will stop pushing him or her to change.

Conclusion

MANY LOOK BACK over the course of their lives and rank their closeness with their children as their greatest joy, and the disruptions and distance, their greatest heartache. Staying married for the sake of your children is an important and worthwhile endeavor. But it will require you to stretch and nurture yourself in ways that may seem impossible at times.

There will be days when you feel completely desperate and fed up and depressed. There will be nights when you feel bitter and jealous of your friends who are happily married, and of strangers who look as if they are. You'll say rude things to your spouse and your kids, and feel hurt and resentful when they say them to you. Work on it. Accept it. Don't freak out. Don't bring out your well-practiced list of deprivations and self-justifications. In the wise words of the recovery movement, live one day at a time.

It's a confusing period in history to be married. On the one hand, marriages have a greater potential for equality and interdependence than in any other time. We have access to an almost infinite amount of information on how to make our marriages stronger, sexier, wealthier, and wiser. People can now end marriages that might have condemned them to a life of abuse or misery during other periods of history. On the other hand, we are faced with a host of social and economic forces which strain our capacity to have good marriages. We feel overworked, underpaid, and starved for attention and nurturance. We're daily seduced into believing that marriage should be as constantly exciting and rewarding as a trip to an exotic country (often, where the residents have more realistic expectations of marriage).

While the marital self-help literature provides many excellent strategies for improving marriage, the economic forces that destroy marriages are scarcely considered by self-help authors or government officials. Those politicians who seem the most intent on getting votes by loudly proclaiming the sanctity of marriage seem the least committed to protecting the programs that will safeguard family stability. There is solid research to show that social policies like those practiced throughout many European (Scandinavian) countries protect a family's ability to remain intact. Almost no government there has significantly cut back on its generous maternal and child benefits despite a global recession. Our assumption that Europe can no longer afford its investment in family care isn't shared by most Europeans. In elections in France and Norway several years ago, politicians competed over how to *increase* governmental support for families (Crittenden 2001). An American politician who ran for office on that platform would be laughed out of the country.

While there are those who blame divorced parents, gay and lesbian parents, single mothers, and unwed mothers for the social ills of today, it seems more reasonable to look at the social deterioration caused by a culture that grants the marketplace the same standing as a religious deity. When corporations here announce layoffs of thousands of employees, they're permitted to do so without regard to how those plant closings will affect the families of those employees, or the towns where they live. This is far less the case in many of the other industrialized countries, where laborers typically sit on the same board as executives and have a direct influence over who will be affected by layoffs and how they will occur.[1]

In the United States, more and more employers are demanding nonstandard work schedules, which are disruptive to family life.

Married couples with children who work rotating shifts and night shifts are at a higher risk for separation or divorce than those with more stable work schedules. These demands are especially difficult for the working poor because they have to devote 35 percent of their income to child care.[2]

Unemployment and poverty are powerful determinants of divorce.[3] The University of Michigan Panel Study of Income Dynamics found that poor families were twice as likely to divorce as others. (Coontz 1992). The Minnesota Family Investment Program found that marriage rates increased for both single-parent long-term recipients and two-parent families when the earnings of employed welfare families were subsidized (Hochschild 2002). It is clear that we need a cultural and economic shift in priorities if couples are going to be able to give their children the security and safety that they need. As sociologist Stephanie Coontz writes in *The Way We Never Were,* "Just as most business ventures could never get off the ground, were it not for public investment in the social overhead capital that subsidizes their transportation and communication, parents need an infrastructure of education, health services, and social support networks to supplement the personal dedication and private resources they invest in childrearing."

Unfortunately, our social infrastructure is rarely given the same priority that we give to other entities. In the past year, we have slashed funds for maternal and child health grants, class-size reduction, early learning, emergency medical services for children, hospital insurance for the uninsured, newborn and infant hearing screening, and mental-health programs (Hochschild 2002). According to a United Nations survey of 152 countries, the United States is one of just six countries that doesn't have a national policy requiring paid maternity leave (Coontz 1992).

Economic security is important to marital harmony, since money is one of the more common things about which couples argue. However, whether the issue is finances, sex, or simple boredom, each person has to decide the best way to proceed with his or her life and marriage. If you are seriously considering divorce, you want to be able to tell your children (and yourself) that you tried everything possible to work it out and you couldn't.

While I'm an eternal optimist, time doesn't always heal all. Time can cause people to change and grow in ways that sometimes move them apart rather than bring them together. We all know people who stayed married into their senior years whose lives together seemed as suffocating as the air in Sylvia Plath's bell jar.

On the other hand, people who impulsively end their marriages feel more vulnerable to accusations from themselves and their children that they didn't try long or hard enough. While time doesn't heal all, it creates the *possibility* for your marriage to change for the better. Divorce buries that possibility once and for all. If my wife and I had divorced when our children were young, we would never have known that we were going to someday successfully resolve what seemed like insurmountable conflicts. Rather than ridding ourselves of our differences with divorce, our problems would have remained frozen there, each of us justifying the other's limitations as a way to rationalize our choice, and anesthetize whatever guilt, sadness, or regret we had about the marriage ending.

There are times in many, if not most, marriages when one or both members of a couple consider separating. A friend of mine recently told me that she was miserable for the first fifteen years of her marriage. "I basically held on for dear life for many, many years because I couldn't afford to move out. I had my kids going in and out of rehab one by one, and my husband and I fought just about every week. If anybody could justify getting out of a marriage, it would have been me. But, at some point, it just got easier. If you had told me back then that someday I would be happily married to the same person, I would've asked you how much crack you had smoked before you looked into your crystal ball."

Sometimes, it really *is* a matter of hanging in there long enough or working on it until things change sufficiently so it's manageable; your kids get older, your partner mellows out, you get a new perspective, a crisis abates. Not infrequently, this is a matter of years rather than months. But, given your options, it may be the best solution. Sometimes life only hands us two hard choices. There is a Chinese saying that goes, "When you are trying to run from a problem, sometimes you meet a worse fate down the road."

Studies of breast cancer survivors show that women who have the greatest joy for living and an optimistic view toward life live the longest (Seligman 1991). Recent studies show that these qualities predict longevity for others as well (Seligman 2000; Singer and Ryff 1999; Peterson et al. 1988; Vaillant 2000). Joy in living comes from the quality of your friendships, your relationships with your children, and your connection to your community. It comes from having meaningful work, or interests, or a spiritual life. It comes from an ability to take great pleasure in small things.

Having a good marriage can help. However, if your marriage doesn't make you happy, then it's important to stop looking for your happiness there. Staying together for the sake of your children isn't just for them. It's also something that you do for yourself. Your children won't live with you forever. But your memories of your life with them will.

Acknowledgments

I am grateful to have had the opportunity to write this book. I would like to thank my agent, Felicia Eth, for her interest. Her warmth, enthusiasm, and knowledge of the publishing world were invaluable in helping me find a good home for my book. My editor at St. Martin's Press, Heather Jackson, was a wise and helpful voice throughout the development, and earned my affection early on by forbidding me to take my manuscript on vacation. It was also her idea to expand the book from one focused on couples in distressed marriages, to one that encompasses the state of the institution today.

I am also grateful to my teachers Joseph Weiss, M.D., Hal Sampson, Ph.D., William Dickman, M.D., and Jamie Edmund, Ph.D. I learned how to be a therapist from them through private consultations, case conferences, and research group meetings. Their kindness, humor, intelligence, and dedication to their patients remain a source of inspiration. I am also indebted to Dr. Weiss for his development of "Control-Mastery Theory" and to my friends and colleagues at the San Francisco Psychotherapy Research Group, led by Dr. Weiss and Dr. Sampson.

I had several people read the manuscript for clarity, organization, and content. I am very grateful to them for generously volunteering their time to help make the book what it is. They are David Auld, Ph.D., Polly Bloomberg-Fretter, Ph.D., Dale Dallas, M.D., Jessica Flynn, M.F.T., Heather Folsom, M.D., Melody Matthews Lowman, M.A., Sandra Marie Ruiz, Lisa Levine, M.F.T., Lori Katzburg, L.C.S.W., and Richard Vogel, Ph.D.

Heartfelt thanks to Jamie Edmund, Ph.D., for our discussions on this topic and for her detailed read of the manuscript. Her considerable expertise in child, couple, and family work was invaluable in helping me develop and refine my thinking in areas that were central to the book's thesis. Deepest thanks also to my friend and colleague Jessica Broitman, Ph.D., for her many readings and critiques. Her expertise in child and adult psychology was a tremendous addition. Thanks also to Michael Simon, M.F.T., who brought his intelligence and organizational expertise.

My friend Heidi Swillinger gets the award for ?rites Read," for which I am forever indebted, especially since she won't let me pick up the tab at dinner. She not only read the manuscript at every stage of development, but read every chapter rewrite. This book is so much stronger because I received the benefit of her fine editorial eye. Thank you, thank you, thank you.

My friends for being my friends. You rule.

My parents, for being good parents, and for having a healthy, enduring marriage. I am grateful for their love, humor, and friendship. My father, a former columnist, for his editing of the manuscript.

To my wonderful children, Misha, Max, and Daniel.

And last and never least, to my wife, Ellie Schwartman, Ph.D., who has been my editor, friend, and adviser throughout this process. For teaching me the meaning of love and commitment.

Notes

INTRODUCTION

1. It is common for therapists and parents to believe that if the adults aren't happy in the marriage, then the children must be unhappy. In the past thirty to forty years, this has caused many to *leave* marriages, believing (at least in part) that they were doing it for the sake of their children. However, as Wallerstein, Lewis, and Blakeslee (2000) observe from their twenty-five-year study of divorce, parental unhappiness isn't always correlated with child unhappiness. They write, "Indeed, many adults who are trapped in unhappy marriages would be surprised to learn that their children are relatively content."

Their findings that children are more likely to be harmed by divorce have been verified in numerous studies (for reviews, see Amato 1993, 2001; Amato and Keith 1991; Cherlin et al. 1991; McLanahan and Sandefur 1994). In a recent metanalysis of the research literature on children of divorce, sociologist Paul Amato (2001) writes, "In the 1990's, as in earlier decades, research indicated that children with divorced parents scored significantly lower than children with continuously married parents on a variety of measures." These include academic achievement, psychological adjustment, well-being, self-concept, and difficulties with interpersonal relationships. Amato noted that the negative effects of divorce appear to have increased in the past decade rather than decreased.

While there is an ongoing debate about whether the negative effects of divorce for children are due to family processes that occurred prior to the divorce or to the loss of social and financial capital that occurs with divorce, *both* appear to contribute and to have independent negative effects on the well-being of children (Amato 2001; Hanson 1999).

Some studies, such as Hetherington (2002), find that children of divorce do as well as children from nondivorced households three out of four times. Her findings, discussed in *For Better or Worse: Divorce Reconsidered,* are a nuanced portrait of marriage and divorce, and have been useful for my writings in this book. However, I don't agree with the conclusion that a 20–25 percent incidence of problems stemming from divorce is a lesson in resilience. As she observes, this is an incidence of problems that is more than double that of the nondivorced population (the statistic goes up to 38 percent when children are exposed to multiple divorces). In addition, this resilience only begins to emerge after some six years of emotional turmoil as the children reckon with the changes caused by the divorce.

A recent study by Lauman-Billings and Emery (2000) showed that the "resilience" conclusion may be an artifact of how we evaluate psychological functioning. They found that while their sample of adult children of divorce showed a low incidence of diagnosable mental disorders, they showed a significantly *higher* incidence of psychological distress. Greater distress was found among young adult children of divorce around the themes of frequency of contact with fathers, interparental conflict, and place of residence.

2. Numerous studies show that children may benefit from divorce if the marriage is characterized by conflict that is intense, chronic, overt, and unresolved, and if divorce means an end to the conflict (Amato 2001; Amato and Booth 1997; Amato, Loomis, and Booth 1995; Hanson, 1999; Jekielek 1998; Kelly 2000; Morrison and Coiro 1999). In those situations, the offspring look more like those raised in happy, intact homes.

However, high-conflict divorces appear to characterize a minority of couples with children (Amato 2001). Amato and Booth (1997) found that a majority of recent divorces are not preceded by an extended period of intense and overt conflict. Gottman (1994) found that fewer than 40 percent of divorces are preceded by frequent and devastating fights. As a result, many may be terminating a marriage more for reasons of personal growth than because the relationship is harmful to their children (Booth 1999; Glenn 1996 in Amato 2001). These are troubling findings because while the parents sometimes benefit from divorce, there is evidence that children may be especially harmed when the marriage is characterized by low conflict (Amato 2001; Amato, Loomis, and Booth 1995; Hanson 1999; Jekielek 1998; Morrison and Coiro 1999). Marriages that are characterized by "encapsulated conflict" such as marital apathy or indifference have not been associated with problems in children (Grych and Fincham 1990).

3. Amato and Booth (1997) found that "relations with parents appear to suffer on average, more when parents divorce than when unhappily married parents stay together. The exception to this trend involves same-gender parent-child ties in divorces that occur when children are older" (pps. 77–78). Aquilino (1994) found that remarriage lessened the offspring's contact with custodial parents regardless of parent's gender (in Amato and Booth 1997 and Booth 1997.

1. MARRIAGE UNDER PRESSURE

1. Hetherington's research (2002) shows that traditional marriages work well as long as both partners share the same view of their gender roles and gain meaning from those roles. In addition, Amato and Booth (1997) found no difference in adult satisfaction or adjustment between those raised in traditional versus nontraditional homes.

2. Crittenden (2001) compares American mothers to Swedish mothers, who are more likely to have governmental supports for child care, which allows them to maintain career goals while being parents. She writes in *The Price of Motherhood*, "Since most mothers also work [in Sweden], the standard of living of women and their children declines by only about 10 percent after the parents divorce. With the weight of the law behind her, a woman who decides that her marriage is unsatisfactory is in a better position to do something about it. She can ask her husband to change, to do more housework and child care for example. Or she can end the marriage without paying too high a financial price." See also Christopher (2002).

3. Hochschild (1997) notes that 74 percent of working mothers have children six to seventeen, 59 percent have children six and under, and 55 percent have kids one and under.

4. This is a troubling phenomenon given Amato and Booth's finding (1997) that children felt much more affection later in life toward fathers who were involved in child care than toward those who weren't.

5. Barich and Bielby (1996) in Amato and Booth (1997). Sociologist Stephanie Coontz (1992) writes in *The Way We Never Were*, "The expectation that the family should be the main source of personal fulfillment was not traditional in the eighteenth and nineteenth centuries. . . . Only in the twentieth century did the family come to be the center of festive attention and emotional intensity."

6. Hetherington (2002). Gottman (1994) writes, "While the wife is embracing a new sense of 'we-ness' that includes the child, the husband may still be pining for the old 'us.'"

7. Cowley (2002). Or as editor and author Lewis Lapham wrote (1988) in *Money and Class in America: Notes and Observations on the Civil Religion*, "What interests me is the cramped melancholy habitual among a citizenry that proclaims itself the happiest and freest ever to have bestrode the earth. Never in the history of the world have so many people been so rich; never in the history of the world have so many of those same people felt themselves so poor."

2. THE HOPED-FOR MARRIAGE

1. Gottman (1994). He estimates that distressed couples underestimate this as much as 50 percent of the time.

2. For a discussion on the effect of parental conflict and of yelling at children see Cummings and Cummings (1988).

3. For exercises to combat negative forecasting and catastrophic thinking, see Burns (1999).

4. Joan Kelly (2000) writes, "The presence of conflict and verbal disagreement between parents is not in itself a reliable predictor of child adjustment, and the threshold at which risk occurs in each family is unknown. Conflict between parents is common in resolving important child-rearing disputes and financial disputes, and some parents and ethnic groups have a familial style of loud, argumentative discussions." See also Grych and Fincham (1990).

5. Weiss and Sampson (1986); Weiss (1993). See Engel and Ferguson (1990) for a good self-help book that explicates Weiss's theories, and the research of Weiss, Sampson, and the San Francisco Psychotherapy Research Group.

3. MESSAGES FROM THE PAST

1. Anthropologist Sara Hrdy (1999) writes that infants likely evolved this capacity because throughout much of our evolution, those infants that could connect with a mother had a better chance of being protected by that parent. "Babies right after birth are at the greatest risk of maternal abandonment or infanticide. . . . Human mothers are far more likely to abandon their infants than are other primates who give birth to one baby at a time." See also Daniel Stern (1990), *Diary of a Baby,* for a discussion of a newborn's abilities to observe and relate to the parent. Also Pinker (2002).

2. I am indebted to Dr. Joseph Weiss and the research of the San Francisco Psychotherapy Research Group led by Dr. Weiss and Dr. Hal Sampson for many of the themes and ideas discussed in this chapter. I am also indebted to the writings of Dr. Jeffrey Young and Dr. Janet Klosko.

3. For a good discussion of how these feelings can affect the intimate and sexual realm, see David Schnarch's *The Sexual Crucible: An Integration of Marital and Sexual Therapy* (1991) and *Passionate Marriage: Love, Sex, Intimacy in Emotionally Committed Relationships* (1998).

4. Coontz (1992) writes, "No other minority got so few payoffs for sending its children to school, and no other immigrants ran into such a low ceiling that college graduates had to become Pullman porters. No other minority was saddled with such unfavorable demographics during early migration, inherited such a deteriorating stock of housing, or was so completely excluded from industrial work during the main heyday of its expansion. And no other minority experienced the extreme hypersegregation faced by blacks until the present."

4. STARTING TO CHANGE

1. As an example, Diamond (1993) cites a study where researchers sprayed perfume on the vagina and nipples of mother rats before they gave birth and during the period of nursing. Researchers found that when these baby rats reached maturity, they were far more attracted to perfumed rats of the opposite sex for mating than they were nonperfumed rats.

5. DEPRESSION IN MARRIAGE

1. Child abuse may retard development of the amygdala, an area of the brain involved in creating the emotional content of memories such as aggressive responses or feelings related to fear conditioning. Because women are twice as likely to be victims of sexual abuse, this likely contributes to the higher levels of depression rates reported in them. See also Damasio (1999), Leibenluft (1998).

2. Tannen (1990). Sociologist Steven Goldberg (1973, in Fisher 1992) writes that men more regularly give up time, pleasure, health, safety, affection, and relaxation to attain positions of rank, authority, and power out of their biological drive to acquire rank. Other evidence for this argument was a study showing that men produced one and one-half times the amount of serotonin as women (in Leibenluft 1998). This finding is supported by primate research where it was found that leaders had one and one-half the amount of serotonin as other troop members. Elevated levels of serotonin have been positively associated with increased rank. In addition, if this leader was pulled from the group and his serotonin was reduced, he lost his leadership (in Lewis, Amini, and Lannon 2000).

6. SEX

1. However, parental good intentions are no insurance that a child benefits from this behavior. All parents make mistakes, and sometimes the mistakes that are made come from trying to repair or replace what was missing or present in the parent's childhood. Thus, a parent who was overly controlled may be overly permissive with his children; a parent who was neglected may be intrusive and excessively involved when she becomes a parent. For a discussion of this and related issues, see Coleman (2000b).

2. Remarriages have a 60 percent probability of divorce according to Gottman (1994).

3. Women may be more vulnerable to worrying and preoccupation than men. See Nolen-Hoeksema, Grayson, and Larson (1999).

4. Women are more likely to view a good sex life as only one of several criteria, along with good communication, affection, and trustworthiness, according to Gottman (1999), Hetherington (2002), and Hrdy (1999).

5. I am indebted to Dr. Janis Spring (1997) for her writings on the subject of affairs.

7. THE HIGH-CONFLICT MARRIAGE

1. Amato and Booth (1997). Hetherington (2002) writes "Even if they visit regularly and are skilled, non-residential parents occupy too little emotional shelf space in the life of a child to provide a reliable buffer against a custodial parent who goes into free fall."

2. Ahrons (1994). Hetherington (2002) notes that the rate of failure of remarriages is 50 percent higher for those with stepchildren than for those without.

3. Hetherington (2002) describes four common fantasies that promote problematic stepfamily interactions; the *nuclear family myth*, the *compensation myth*, the *instant love expectation*, and the *rescue fantasy*. Understanding how these expectations may be affecting your marriage may help you reduce the conflict in your household.

    In the *nuclear family myth*, the marriage is stressed by one or both members of the couple believing that the stepfamily will have the same kind of togetherness and shared loyalties as the nonstepfamily. This is almost always a problem because stepfamilies frequently have competing loyalties for time, attention, and financial resources.

    The *compensation myth* is characterized by a belief that a new spouse will make up for what was missing in the first spouse. A woman who left her husband because of his emotional unavailability may be even more angry or upset when her second husband begins to show these traits. A man who left his first wife because of her lack of vitality may resent or criticize his second wife even more if she shows a similar tendency.

    In the *instant love expectation* there is the irrational belief that a stepchild will or should feel close to a stepparent before a relationship has been established (that is, if the stepchildren will *allow* a close relationship to be established). In addition, there is the often problematic belief that a stepparent has the right to become a parental authority with a child before he or she has developed the kind of intimacy and trust that gives that authority credibility.

    The *rescue fantasy* is when a stepparent believes that he or she will rescue the children from a difficult biological parent. It can also result from a stepparent who wants to rescue the new spouse from difficult kids.

8. IS CHANGE POSSIBLE?

1. I am indebted to Dr. John Gottman (1994, 1999) for his research and writing on helping couples change.

2. Gottman's research shows that couples who are happily married have a ratio of five positive interactions for every negative.

3. I am indebted to Dr. Susan Forward (1987, 1997) for her ideas about helping individuals who live in high-conflict marriages.

4. For good examples see Bourne (2000), Beck (1988), or Burns (1999). For a good discussion of the role of the unconscious in producing and maintaining pathogenic beliefs see Weiss and Sampson (1986), Weiss (1993).

5. John Gottman's research (1994) shows that people get physiologically activated during conflict and that this directly interferes with their capacity to be rational or cooperative. He found that a pulse rate ten beats per minute above normal is sufficiently high to negatively affect communication!

CONCLUSION

1. Greider (1997). See also Karen Christopher (2002), who writes, "The high poverty rate of U.S. women is due to two main factors: the prevalence of poverty-wage jobs and the failure of the government's welfare programs to pull its citizens out of poverty. American women and single mothers are the most likely to earn poverty-level wages. When working full time (at least 35 hours a week), about one third of U.S. women and more than 40 percent of U.S. single mothers earn wages too low to free their families from poverty."

2. Hochschild (2002); Christopher (2002). In addition, as policy analyst Theodora Ooms (2002) writes, "It's not just the case that single mothers find themselves poor because they are unmarried; they find themselves unmarried because they are poor. Successful marriages are more difficult when husbands and wives are poorly educated, lack access to jobs that pay decently, and cannot afford decent child care."

3. Coontz (1992) goes on to say, "America spends proportionately less on such social investments than does almost any other major industrial country. . . . If there is any pattern to be found in the variety of families that have succeeded and failed over the course of history it is that children do best in societies where childrearing is considered too important to be left entirely to parents."

References

Ahrons, Constance. 1994. *The Good Divorce: Keeping Your Family Together When Your Marriage Comes Apart.* New York: HarperCollins.

———. 2002. "Couples at the Crossroads." Workshop at the Love and Intimacy Couples Conference, April 20.

Alman, Isadora. 2002. Telephone conversation, February 8, San Francisco.

Amato, Paul R. 1994. "Life-Span Adjustment of Children to Their Parents' Divorce." *Future Child* 4: 143–64.

———. 2001. "Children of Divorce in the 1990s: An Update of the Amato and Keith (1991) Meta-analysis." *Journal of Family Psychology* 15(3) (September): 355–70.

Amato, Paul R., and B. Keith. 1991. "Parental Divorce and the Well-Being of Children: A Meta-analysis." *Psychological Bulletin* 110: 26–46.

Amato, Paul R., Laura Loomis, and Alan Booth. 1995. "Parental Divorce, Parental Marital Conflict, and Offspring Well-Being During Early Adulthood." *Social Forces* 73: 895–916.

Amato, Paul R., and Alan Booth. 1997. *A Generation at Risk.* Cambridge, Mass.: Harvard University Press.

Amstutz-Haws, W., and B. Mallinckrodt. 1996. "Separation-Individuation from Parents and Marital Adjustment in Newlywed Couples." Presentation at the American Psychological Association Convention.

Aquilino, William S. 1994. "Impact of Childhood Family Disruption on Young Adult's Relationship with Parents." *Journal of Marriage and the Family* 56: 296–313.

Bader, Michael J. 2002. *Arousal: The Secret Logic of Sexual Fantasies.* New York: St. Martin's Press.

Barbach, Lonnie. 1976. *For Yourself: The Fulfillment of Female Sexuality.* Garden City, N.Y.: Anchor.

———. 1984. *For Each Other: Sharing Sexual Intimacy.* New York: Signet.

Barich, Rachel R. and Denise D. Bielby. 1996. "Rethinking Marriage: Change and Stability in Expectations, 1967–1994." *Journal of Family Issues* 17: 139–69.

Bateson, Mary C. 2001. "Rethinking Fidelity." *San Francisco Chronicle*, February 11.

Beck, Aaron. 1988. *Love Is Never Enough: How Couples Can Overcome Misunderstandings, Resolve Conflicts, and Solve Relationship Problems Through Cognitive Therapy.* New York: Harper and Row.

Belsky, J., L. Youngblade, M. Rovine, and B. Volling. 1991. "Patterns of Marital Change and Parent-Child Interaction." *Journal of Marriage and Family* 53: 487–98.

Belsky, J., and J. Kelly. 1994. *The Transition to Parenthood: How a First Child Changes a Marriage. Why Some Couples Grow Closer Together and Others Apart.* New York: Dell.

Belsky, J., and E. Pensky. 1998. "Marital Change Across the Transition to Parenthood." *Journal of Marriage and the Family* 52: 5–19.

Benazon, Nili R., and James C. Coyne. 2000. "Living with a Depressed Spouse." *Journal of Family Psychology* 14 (1): 71–79.

Benson, Herbert. 1985. *Beyond the Relaxation Response.* New York: Berkeley.

Berman, Jennifer, and Laura Berman. 2001. *For Women Only: A Revolutionary Guide to Overcoming Sexual Dysfunction and Reclaiming Your Sex Life.* New York: Henry Holt.

Bird, C. E. 1999. "Gender, Household, and Psychological Disease: The Impact of the Amount and Division of Housework." *Journal of Health and Social Behavior* 40: 32–45.

Black, Claudia. 1981. *It Will Never Happen to Me.* New York: Ballantine.

Blumstein, Philip, and Pepper Schwartz. 1983. *American Couples: Money, Work, Sex.* New York: William Morrow.

Bowen, Murray. 1978. *Family Therapy in Clinical Practice.* New York: Jason Aronson.

Bowlby, John. 1953. "Some Pathological Processes Set in Train by Early Mother-Child Separation." *Journal of Mental Science* 99: 265–72.

———. 1972. *Attachment:* Vol. 1. *Attachment and Loss.* Middlesex, England: Penguin.

Bourne, Edmund J. 2000. *The Anxiety and Phobia Workbook.* Oakland, Calif.: New Harbinger.

Brown, G. W., A. Bifulco, H. O. Veiel, and B. Andrews. 1990. "Self-Esteem and Depression: Aetiological Issues." *Social Psychiatry Psychiatric Epidemiology* 25: 235–43.

Burns, David. 1999. *Feeling Good: The New Mood Therapy.* New York: Wholecare.

Cherlin A., F. Furstenberg, L. Chase-Lansdale, et al. 1991. "Longitudinal Studies of Divorce on Children in Great Britain and the United States." *Science* 252: 1386–89.

Christopher, Karen. 2002. "Family-Friendly Europe." *American Prospect*, April.

Cobb, Jonathon, and Richard Sennett. 1972. *The Hidden Injuries of Class.* New York: Knopf.

Coleman, Joshua D. 2000a. "When a Family Man Thinks Twice." *San Francisco Chronicle.* Sunday, June 18.

———. 2000b. "Strangers at Our Table." *San Francisco Chronicle*, Sunday, November 12.

Coontz, Stephanie. 1992. *The Way We Never Were*. New York: Basic Books.

———. 1997. "An Interview with Stephanie Coontz." Salon.com. *http://archive.salon.com/may97/book1970520.html*.

Cousins, S. D. 1989. "Culture and Self-Perception in Japan and the United States." *Journal of Personality and Social Psychology* 56: 124–31.

Cowan, C. P., and P. A. Cowan. 1992. *When Partners Become Parents*. New York: Basic Books.

Cowley, Geoffrey. 2002. The Science of Happiness." *Newsweek*, September 16.

Crittenden, Ann. 2001. *The Price of Motherhood: Why the Most Important Job in the World Is Still the Least Valued*. New York: Henry Holt.

Cross, Susan E., and Laura Madson. 1997. "Models of the Self: Self-Construals and Gender." *Psychological Bulletin* 1222 (1): 5–37.

Cummings, E. Mark, and Jennifer L. Cummings. 1988. "A Process-Oriented Approach to Children's Coping with Adults' Angry Behavior." *Developmental Review* 8: 296–321.

Dadds, M. R., E. Atkinson, C. Turner, G. J. Blums, and B. Lendich. 1999. "Family Conflict and Child Adjustment: Evidence for a Cognitive Contextual Model of Intergenerational Transmission." *Journal of Family Psychology* 13: 194–208.

Damasio, Antonio. 1999. *The Feeling of What Happens: Body and Emotion in the Making of Consciousness*. Orlando, Fla.: Harcourt.

Diagnostic and Statistical Manual of Mental Disorders. 2000. American Psychiatric Press.

Diamond, Jared. 1993. *The Third Chimpanzee*. New York: HarperPerennial.

———. 1997. *Why Is Sex Fun? The Evolution of Human Sexuality*. New York: Basic Books.

William J. Doherty. 1998. "Responsible Fathering: An Overview and Conceptual Framework." *Journal of Marriage and the Family* 60: 277–92.

Doi, Takeo. 1973. *The Anatomy of Dependence*. New York: Harper and Row.

Ehrensaft, Diane. 1997. *Spoiling Childhood: How Well-Meaning Parents Are Giving Children Too Much—But Not What They Need*. New York: Guilford Press.

Ellis, A., and A. Harper. 1961. *A Guide to Rational Living*. North Hollywood, Calif.: Wilshire Books.

Emery, Robert E. 1982. "Interparental Conflict and the Children of Discord and Divorce." *Psychological Bulletin* 92: 310–30.

Engel, Lewis, and Tom Ferguson. 1991. *Hidden Guilt*. New York: Pocket Books.

Etcoff, Nancy. 2000. *Survival of the Prettiest*. New York: Anchor.

Fisher, Helen. 1992. *Anatomy of Love: A Natural History of Monogamy, Adultery and Divorce*. New York: Simon and Schuster.

Forward, Susan. 1987. *Men Who Hate Women and the Women Who Love Them*. New York: Bantam.

———. 1997. *Emotional Blackmail: When the People in Your Life Use Fear, Obligation, and Guilt to Manipulate You*. New York: HarperPerennial.

Freud, Sigmund. 1918. *Totem and Taboo*. Translated by A. A. Brill. New York: Moffat, Yard.

———. 1926. "Inhibitions, Symptoms, and Anxiety." Standard Edition 20, 77–175. London: Hogarth Press.

Fuchs, Victor. 1988. *Women's Quest for Economic Equality.* Cambridge, Mass.: Harvard University Press.

Gilligan, Carol. 1982. *In a Different Voice: Psychological Theory and Women's Development.* Cambridge, Mass.: Harvard University Press.

Glenn, N. 1991. "The Recent Trend in Marital Success in the United States." *Journal of Marriage and the Family* 53: 261–70.

———. 1996. "Values, Attitudes, and the State of the American Marriage." *Promises to Keep: Decline and Renewal of Marriage in America,* edited by D. Popenoe, J. B. Elshtain, and D. Blankenhorn. Lanham, Md.: Rowman and Littlefield.

Goethals, G., D. M. Messick, and S. T. Allison. 1991. "The Uniqueness Bias: Studies of Constructive Social Comparison." In *Social Comparison: Contemporary Theory and Research,* edited by J. Suls and I. A. Wills. Hillsdale, N.J.: Erlbaum.

Goldberg, Steven. 1973. *The Inevitability of Patriarchy.* New York: William Morrow.

Gottman, John. 1994. *Why Marriages Succeed or Fail . . . and How You Can Make Yours Last.* New York: Simon and Schuster.

———. 1999. *The Seven Principles for Making Marriage Work.* New York: Crown.

Greider, William. 1997. *One World, Ready or Not: The Manic Logic of Global Capitalism.* New York: Touchstone.

Grych, John H., and Frank D. Fincham. 1990. "Marital Conflict and Children's Adjustment: A Cognitive Contextual Framework." *Psychological Bulletin* 108: 267–90.

Hammen, C. I., and S. D. Peters. 1978. "Interpersonal Consequences of Depression: Responses to Men and Women Enacting a Depressed Role." *Journal of Abnormal Psychology* 87: 322–32.

Hanson, T. L. 1999. "Does Parental Conflict Explain Why Divorce Is Negatively Associated with Child Welfare?" *Social Forces* 77: 1283–1316.

Hendrix, Harville. 1988. *Getting the Love You Want: A Guide for Couples.* New York: HarperPerennial.

Hetherington, E. Mavis. 2002. "Marriage and Divorce American Style." *American Prospect,* April.

Hetherington, E. Mavis, and John Kelly. 2002. *For Better or Worse: Divorce Reconsidered.* New York: W. W. Norton.

Hochschild, Arlie. 1989. *The Second Shift.* New York: Avon.

———. 1997. *The Time Bind: When Work Becomes Home and Home Becomes Work.* New York: Henry Holt.

———. 2002. "Taking Care." *American Prospect,* April.

Hofer, M. A. 1984. "Relationships as Regulators: A Psychobiologic Perspective on Bereavement." *Psychosomatic Medicine* 46 (3): 183–97.

Hrdy, Sara Blaffer. 1999. *Mother Nature: Maternal Instincts and How They Shape the Human Species.* New York: Ballantine.

Jack, Dana Crowley. 1991. *Silencing the Self: Women and Depression.* New York: HarperPerennial.

Jeffers, Susan. 1987. *Fear the Fear and Do It Anyway.* San Diego: Harcourt.

Jekielek, Susan M. 1998. "Parental Conflict, Marital Disruption and Children's Emotional Well-Being." *Social Forces* 76: 905–35

Jordan, J. V., and J. L. Surrey. 1986. "The Self-in-Relation: Empathy and the Mother-Daughter Relationship." In *The Psychology of Today's Women*, edited by T. Bernay and D. W. Cantor. Cambridge, Mass.: Guilford Press.

Keitner, G. I., and J. W. Miller. 1990. "Family Functioning and Major Depression: An Overview." *American Journal of Psychiatry* 147: 1128–37.

Kelly, Joan B. 2000. "Children's Adjustment in Conflicted Marriage and Divorce: A Decade Review of Research." *Journal of the American Academy of Child and Adolescent Psychiatry* 39: 8.

Kiecolt-Glaser, K. Janet, and Tamara L. Newton. 2001. "Marriage and Health: His and Hers." *Psychological Bulletin* 127: 472–503.

Kierkegaard, Søren. 1959 [1843]. "The Rotation Method: An Essay in the Theory of Social Prudence." In *Either/Or*, vol. 1. Princeton N.J.: Princeton University Press, 279–96.

———. 1998 [1847]. *Works of Love*. Vol. 16 of *Kierkegaard's Writings*. Edited by Howard V. Hong and Edna H. Hong. Princeton, N.J.: Princeton University Press.

Kramer, Peter. 1993. *Listening to Prozac*. New York: Penguin.

———. 1997. *Should You Leave?* New York: Penguin.

Kübler-Ross, Elisabeth. 1969. *Death and Dying*. New York: Macmillan.

Lapham, Lewis. 1988. *Money and Class in America: Notes and Observations on the Civil Religion*. New York: Random House.

Laumann-Billings, Lisa, and Robert E. Emery 2000. "Distress Among Young Adults from Divorced Families." *Journal of Family Psychology* 14(4) (December): 671–87.

Lawson, Annette. 1988. *Adultery: An Analysis of Love and Betrayal*. New York: Basic Books.

Lederer, William J., and Don D. Jackson. 1968. *The Mirages of Marriage*. New York: W. W. Norton.

Leibenluft, Ilen. 1998. "Teens and 20s: Why Are So Many Women Depressed?" *Scientific American*.

LeShan, Lawrence 1974. *How to Meditate*. New York: Bantam Books.

Lewis, Thomas, Amini Fari, and Richard Lannon. 2000. *A General Theory of Love*. New York: Random House.

Lowman, Melody. 2002. Conversation April, 25, San Francisco.

Markus, H. R., and S. Kitayama. 1991. "Culture and the Self: Implications for Cognition, Emotion, and Motivation." *Psychological Review* 98: 224–53.

Markus, H. R., P. R. Mullally, and S. Kitayama. 1997. "Selfways: Diversity in Modes of Cultural Participation." In *The Conceptual Self in Context*, edited by U. Neisser and D. Jopling. New York: Cambridge University Press.

Masters, William, A., Virginia E. Johnson and C. Robert Kolodny. *Heterosexuality*. 1994. New York: HarperCollins.

McLanahan, Sara S., and Gary Sandefur. 1994. *Growing Up with a Single Parent: What Hurts, What Helps*. Cambridge, Mass., Harvard University Press.

Miller, Alice. 1981. *The Drama of the Gifted Child: How Narcissistic Parents Form and Deform the Emotional Lives of Their Talented Children*. New York: Harper and Row.

———. 1990. *For Your Own Good: Hidden Cruelty in Child-Rearing and the Roots of Violence*. New York: Noonday Press.

Morrison, D. R., and M. J. Coiro. 1999. "Parental Conflict and Marital Disruption: Do Children Benefit When High Conflict Marriages Are Dissolved?" *Journal of Marriage and the Family* 61: 626–37.

Murray, L. 1992. "The Impact of Postnatal Depression on Infant Development." *Journal of Child Psychology and Psychiatry and Allied Disciplines* 33 (3): 543–61.

Murray, L. P., P. J. Cooper and A. Stein. 1991. "Postnatal Depression and Infant Development." *British Medical Journal* 302 (63): 978–9.

Nathanson, Donald. 1992. *Shame and Pride: Affect, Sex and the Birth of the Self.* New York: W. W. Norton.

Neighbors, B., R. Forehand, and D. McVicar 1993. "Resilient Adolescents and Interparental Conflict." *American Journal of Orthopsychiatry* 63: 462–71.

Nelson, Noelle. 2001. *Dangerous Relationships: How to Identify and Respond to the Seven Warning Signs of a Troubled Relationship.* New York: Perseus.

Nolen-Hoeksema, S. and J. S. Girgus. 1994. "The Emergence of Gender Differences in Depression During Adolescence." *Psychological Bulletin* 115: 424–43.

Ooms, Thomas. 2002. "Marriage Plus: Most People Agree That It's Healthy to Grow Up in a Two-Person Family. But the Marriage Contract Is Just the Beginning." *American Prospect*, April.

Ostrander, Susan. 1984. *Women of the Upper Class.* Philadelphia: Temple University Press.

Peled, E., G. Eisikovits, G. Enosh, and Z. Winstok. 2000. "Choice and Empowerment for Battered Women Who Stay: Toward a Constructivist Model." *Social Work* 45(1) (January): 9–24.

Person, Ethel Spector. 1988. *Dreams of Love and Fateful Encounters: The Power of Romantic Passion.* New York: W. W. Norton.

Peterson, C., M. E. P. Seligman, K. H. Yurko, L. R. Martin, and H. S. Friedman. 1988. "Pessimistic Explanatory Style Is a Risk Factor for Physical Illness: A Thirty-Five-Year Longitudinal Study." *Journal of Personality and Social Psychology* 55: 23–27.

Phillipson, C. 1997. "Social Relationships in Later Life: A Review of the Research Literature." *International Journal of Geriatric Psychiatry* 12:505–12.

Pittman, Frank. 1989. *Private Lies.* New York: W. W. Norton.

Pleck, J. H. 1997. "Paternal Involvement: Levels, Sources, and Consequences." In *The Role of the Father in Child Development,* 3rd ed., Lamb, ML: Wiley.

Plomin, R., D. Reiss, E. M. Hetherington, and G. W. Howe. "Nature and Nurture: Genetic Contributions to Measures of the Family Environment." *Developmental Psychology* 30: 32–43.

Popenoe, David. 1996. *Life Without Father: Compelling New Evidence That Fatherhood and Marriage Are Indispensable for the Good of Children and Society.* Cambridge Mass.: Harvard University Press.

Pruett, Kyle. 2000. *Fatherneed: Why Father Care Is As Essential As Mother Care for Your Child.* Free Press.

Real, Terrence. 1997. *I Don't Want to Talk About It.* New York: Scribner.

———. 2002. *How Can I Get Through to You?* New York: Scribner.

Reiss, D. 1995. "Genetic Influence on Family Systems: Implications for Development." *Journal of Marriage and the Family* 57: 543–60.

Roberston, R., L. Rooke, and H. T. Teng. 1986. "Gender Effects on Social Participation: Intimacy, Loneliness, and the Conduct of Social Interaction." In *The Emerging Field of Personal Relationships*, edited by R. Gilmour and S. Duck. Hillsdale, N.J.: Erlbaum.

Rosen, Laura Epstein, and Xavier Francisco Amador. 1996. *When Someone You Love Is Depressed: How to Help Your Loved One Without Losing Yourself.* New York: Fireside.

Schnarch, David. 1991. *The Sexual Crucible: An Integration of Marital and Sexual Therapy.* New York: W. W. Norton.

———. 1998. *Passionate Marriage: Love, Sex, Intimacy in Emotionally Committed Relationships.* New York: Henry Holt.

Schwartzman, Ellen. 2002. Conversation March 2, Oakland, Calif.

Seligman, Martin. 1991. *Learned Optimism: How to Change Your Mind and Your Life.* New York: Knopf.

———. Martin. 2000. "Optimism, Pessimism and Mortality." *Mayo Clinical Proceedings* 75: 133–34.

Seligman, M. F. P., C. Peterson, N. J. Kaslow, R. L. Tannenbaum, L. B. Alloy, and L. Y. Abramson. 1984. "Explanatory Style and Depressive Symptoms Among Young Children." *Journal of Abnormal Psychology* 93: 235–38.

Singer, B., and C. D. Ryff. 1999. "Hierarchies of Life Histories and Associated Health Risks." *Annals of the New York Academy of Sciences* 896: 96–115.

Spring, Janis Abrahms. 1997. *After the Affair: Healing the Pain and Rebuilding Trust When A Partner Has Been Unfaithful.* New York: HarperPerennial.

Shostak, M. 1981. *Nisa: The Life and Words of a !Kung Woman.* New York: Random House.

Spino, M. 1979. *Beyond Jogging: The Inner Space of Running.* New York: Pocket Books.

Stern, Daniel. 1990. *Diary of a Baby.* New York: Basic Books.

Szabo, A., E. Billet, and J. Turner. 2001. "Phenylethylamine, a Possible Link to the Antidepressant Effect of Exercise?" *British Journal of Sports Medicine.* 35 (5) (October). 342–34.

Tannen, Deborah. 1990. *You Just Don't Understand.* New York: Ballantine Books.

Teicher, Martin. 2002. "The Neurobiology of Child Abuse: Maltreatment at an Early Age Can Have Enduring Negative Effects on a Child's Brain Development and Function." *Scientific American*, March.

Thompson, Keith. 2002. "Battered Men: Research Reveals a Secret Side of Domestic Violence—Women Are Doing the Abusing Too." *Pacific Sun*, July 31–August 6.

University of California. 2001. "Marital Assets." *Berkeley Wellness Newsletter*, vol. 18, issue 1.

Vaillant, G. E. 2000. "Adaptive Mental Mechanisms: Their Role in a Positive Psychology." *American Psychologist* 55: 89–98.

Visher, Emily B., and John S. Visher. 1979. *Stepfamilies: Myths and Realities.* New York: Citadel.

Vogel, Richard. 1994. "The Origins and Resolution of Marital Discord from a Control Mastery Perspective." *Journal of Couples Therapy* 4 (3–4): 47–63.

Waite, Linda. 2002. *Does Divorce Make People Happier? Findings from a Study of Unhappy Couples.* New York: Institute for American Values.

Waite, Linda J., and Maggie Gallagher. 2000. *The Case for Marriage*. New York: Doubleday.

Walker, Lenore (1984). *The Battered Woman Syndrome*. New York, NY: Springer Press.

Wallerstein, Judith S., and Sandra Blakeslee. 1989. *Second Chances: Men, Women, and Children a Decade After Divorce*. New York: Ticknor and Fields.

Wallerstein, Judith S., Julia M. Lewis, and Sandra Blakeslee. 2000. *The Unexpected Legacy of Divorce: A 25-Year Landmark Study*. New York: Hyperion.

Walsh, Anthony. 1991. *The Science of Love: Understanding Love and Its Effects on Mind and Body*. Buffalo, N.Y.: Prometheus.

Warhol, Andy. 1988. *The Philosophy of Andy Warhol: From A to B and Back Again*. New York: Harvest Books.

Weiss, Joseph. 1993. *How Psychotherapy Works: Process and Technique*. New York: Guilford Press.

Weiss, Joseph, and Harold Sampson. 1986. *The Psychoanalytic Process*. New York: Guilford Press.

Weissman, M., V. Warner, and P. Wickramaratne. 1997. "Offspring of Depressed Parents: Ten Years Later." *Archives of General Psychiatry* 54: 932–40.

Winnincott, D. W. 1958. *Collected Papers: Through Paediatrics to Psychoanalysis*. London: Tavistock.

Winterson, Jeanette. 1989. *The Passion*. New York: Vintage.

Young, Jeffrey E. 1999. *Cognitive Therapy for Personality Disorders: A Schema-Focused Approach*. Sarasota, Fla.: Professional Resource Press.

Young, Jeffrey E., and Janet S. Klosko. 1994. *Reinventing Your Life*. New York: Dutton.

Zeitlin, Dennis. 1991. "Control-Mastery Theory in Couples Therapy." *Family Therapy* 18 (3): 201–2.

Index